One Direction: Dare to Dream: Life as One Direction

Copyright © 2011 by One Direction

www.harpercollinschildrens.com

Library of Congress Cataloging-in-Publication Data is
available.

ISBN 978-0-06-221342-6
Canadian edition: 978-0-00-748812-4

12 13 14 15 16 LP/RRDJC 10 9 8 7 6 5 4 3 2 1
❖
Originally published by HarperCollins UK in 2011

100% OFFICIAL

DARE TO DREAM LIFE AS ONE DIRECTION

INTRODUCTION

Welcome to our first book! We can hardly believe it.

We've had so much fun writing this and remembering all the crazy, funny and emotional moments we've had so far. And believe us, there have been many. We want to share as much with you as we can, so inside you can read all about the ups and downs, find out how we really get on with each other and discover our big plans for the future.

It's amazing to think about how much has happened in such a short space of time. This time last year we were just starting out on *The X Factor*. Since then we've done loads of traveling, learned a ridiculous amount and made music which we're incredibly proud of and we hope you love.

It's no exaggeration to say we're having the best time of our lives right now, and there's no way that would be happening if it wasn't for you. Thank you for all your unbelievable support. It means the world to us and we love you. Here's to many, many good times to come.

Love,

HARRY STYLES

HAPPY DAYS

I sometimes get flashbacks of when I was a kid, and I think my earliest memories are of being at Disney World when I was about five. Everything seemed so big and fun and I loved it.

The first time I was ever away from my family was when I started going to a nursery called Happy Days. And they were happy days, to be fair. I always got on really well with all the staff, and the lady who owned the center was our babysitter, so I probably got to play with the good toys more than the other kids did. I was pretty well behaved and I didn't get into a lot of trouble or anything. I was more interested in playing than being naughty.

I remember my first day of school pretty clearly. My mom came and sat with me in the class, and then about halfway through the day she left. All the kids were playing together, but some were crying a bit. I felt fine about it and I had a few friends there so I settled in quite quickly and never minded being there. My best friend in primary school was a guy called Jonathan, and he's still a good friend

of mine now and I see him all the time. He came to see me on the tour and we always keep in touch.

I was in the school plays from a really young age and I once played Buzz Lightyear in *Chitty Chitty Bang Bang*. I know that sounds a bit weird, but basically when the children hid from the Child Catcher in the toy store they had Buzz and Woody in there, so I got to dress up as Buzz. That was one of my first ever performances, if you can call it that.

I also did a play called *Barney* about a mouse who lived in a church. I played Barney and I had to wear a pair of my sister's gray tights and a headband with ears on and sing in front of everyone. I like to think I was a good mouse.

I always used to love singing. The first song I knew all the words to was "The Girl of My Best Friend" by Elvis. My dad introduced me to his music, and when I was given a karaoke machine by my granddad, my cousin and I recorded a load of Elvis tracks. I wish I still had them so I could have a listen.

I liked math from an early age because we got to use bricks and cubes and it was quite fun, but as I got older I found it harder, so I got much more into English. I could produce really good pieces of writing and I felt really proud when I got an A for my first ever essay. But I was so easily distracted that I started spending more and more time chatting to friends in class or daydreaming, and sadly I never quite got up to that standard again.

I liked PE too and I played soccer a lot. When I started playing for the local soccer team in goal I made friends from other schools as well, which meant I had a lot of friends. I've always liked being around people and getting to know new people, so I've always had a wide group of friends. Also I used to be friends with girls as well as boys. I wasn't one of those boys who thought girls were smelly and didn't like them; I was kind of friends with everyone.

I got a bit cheekier as time went on, and when I was about eight or nine I started testing the boundaries. I'd often try and get one over on the teachers. I also got much more interested in girls. I only ever got into one fight the whole time I was at school, and that was in primary school. I'm not the type to pick a fight, and if someone had ever tried to start a fight it would make me laugh more than anything.

When I was seven my mom and dad divorced, and that was quite a weird time. I remember crying about it when my parents told me they were splitting up, but after that I was alright. I guess I didn't really get what was going on properly, I was just sad that my parents wouldn't be together any more.

My mom, my older sister Gemma and I left Holmes Chapel and moved farther out into the Cheshire countryside. Our new home was a pub, and my mom became the landlady. There was a boy called Reg living nearby and he was the only other kid in the area, so even though he was my sister's age we used to hang out together all the time. The summer we moved there Reg and I used to go every day to Great Budworth Ice Cream Farm, which was about two miles away. We'd borrow two pounds off our moms and cycle up there and get an ice cream. I can remember that so clearly. It's the same ice cream farm I took all the boys to when they came to stay before Bootcamp. And the ice cream is still as good now.

On the subject of girls, when I was about six I was friends with a girl called Phoebe Fox. Her mom and mine were best friends, and I bought her a teddy bear the same as my one and everything. She was the cutest little girl. I had a few other girlfriends here and there when I was really young, but I didn't have an actual girlfriend until I was 12. Then I went out with a girl called Emilie, and for quite a long time considering how young we were. She's still a good friend of mine now. I was also with a girl called Abi. I guess you could say that she was my first serious girlfriend.

I've been single now since the end of 2009 and I'm fine with that. I'm not consciously looking for a girlfriend, but if I meet someone I like it would be great. I do like being with someone and if the right person came along, then we'd see what happened.

When I was about 12 we moved back to Holmes Chapel, and that's when my mom met my stepdad, Robin. I really liked him and I was always asking her if he was coming over, but she wanted to make really sure that Gemma and I were okay with him being around. She worried about it a lot, so in the end I used to text him and tell him to come over because I thought he was a really cool guy. I've always got on well with him and I still do now.

I was really pleased when Robin proposed to my mom. He did it completely by surprise while they were watching *Coronation Street* on Christmas Eve a few years ago. I was at my girlfriend Abi's house at the time and I remember getting a call from my mom and how happy I was when she told me they were going to be getting married. I'm not sure when they're planning to do it, and even though a few people have suggested this, I don't think it's very likely that One Direction will be playing at the wedding.

My mom and I have always been close. I'm such a mommy's boy. I'm really close to my dad, Des, as well, and he's very supportive of everything I'm doing. I think we're probably quite alike in a lot of ways.

My sister and I have generally got on very well too. I know that a lot of siblings argue, and we had our moments when we were growing up, but we hang out together a lot now and she even came on part of the tour with me.

I've made a few style mistakes in my time, and sadly there is photographic evidence! My hair has changed a lot over the years. It started white-blond and curly when I was born, then went brown and straight, and then started going

ABOVE: **LOOK AT THAT TARANTULA!**
OPPOSITE: **AGE SIX, ON HOLIDAY IN FLORIDA. WHAT AN OUTFIT!**

I LIKE THINGS THAT INVOLVE SKILL AND I LOVE ANYTHING THAT'S A BIT OF A CHALLENGE

curly again when I was 12. So it's been through several phases. The worst thing was probably when I had blond streaks put in it when I was about eight. I thought it was cool when I went into school the day after having it done, but looking back I looked like a douche. I lived in tracksuits, and as all I ever wanted to do was go out on my bike, I guess it fitted in with my image.

I really enjoyed secondary school and I worked pretty hard, but I enjoyed myself as well. Life is all about balance. I played badminton a lot in secondary school. My dad is really good at it, so I got that from him, and I was always really competitive. I liked the fact that it wasn't the most obvious sport to get into, and that you need quite a lot of skill to play it. I like things that involve skill and I love anything that's a bit of a challenge.

At the end of Year Eight I became friends with a guy called Will and he became like my brother. We had the same sense of humor and we got on really well from the word go. He and a friend called Hayden were really keen to start a band, and a guy called Nick had just started to play bass so he joined them too. They wanted to enter a battle of the bands competition at school and they needed a singer, so they asked me to try out.

That was a bit of a shock as I'd only ever sung to myself in the shower or in the car. I knew I could sing a note, but I had no idea how I'd be. But I'd always imagined what it would be like to be in a band, so I started practicing with them. We were always singing "Summer of 69" by Bryan Adams and "Be My Girl" by Jet, so we decided to perform them in the competition.

We were all ready to go and we started filling out the application form, but we didn't have a name and we couldn't think of anything. It got to the day before the show and we had to put something down, so we decided just to go for something completely random. I suggested White Eskimo, and we hadn't thought of anything better, so we wrote it down and from then on that's who we were.

The competition was in the school canteen, and we decided that we were all going to dress in a similar way so we all had white shirts and black ties on. At the time we thought we looked really cool. All of our friends were down at the front of the stage when we sang "Summer of 69," and afterwards this girl came up to me and said, "Where did that come from?" Three finalists were chosen, including us, and we all had to sing again – and we ended up winning, which was amazing. After that we decided to take things a bit more seriously when it came to practicing.

The band changed a bit after the competition because we got a new bassist, and also a guitarist called Jacob. We used to practice every Wednesday after school at Will's house. Then we landed our first gig.

A girl in my school said that her mom was getting married and wanted us to play at the wedding, so we rehearsed solidly for two days. We had a set list of about 25 songs that the bride had chosen, and we learned the lot. We used my stepdad's PA system and we went along and set it all up and it all went really well. We felt like a proper band. We performed a lot of Bob Marley tracks, some acoustic songs, and I also sang "Hallelujah."

One of the guests at the wedding was a music producer, and afterwards he came and spoke to us and told us we were really good. He also said that I reminded him of Mick Jagger, which of course I loved.

We got paid £160 for the gig, which worked out at £40 each. And we got free sandwiches. What more can you ask for? We practiced more and more after that. Will's mom is a TV and radio presenter called Yvette Fielding. She was really supportive, giving us advice and helping us with everything. Now we were serious about carrying the band on and trying to get a deal or something one day.

I had always thought about going in for *The X Factor*, and watching Eoghan Quigg and Lloyd Daniels in 2009 – young guys like me – made me want to do

it even more. I also think that being in front of an audience with the band had given me a taste for performing. I loved being on stage and I wanted to do more and more.

I didn't know if I had what it took, and I was really nervous about actually taking the step and applying, so in the end my mom filled out the application form and sent it off for me – and I'm so grateful she did. I often have those moments when I think, "What if she hadn't done that" or "What if so and so hadn't happened?" I had one the other day when we were all sitting down looking at an article about us. It hit me that if I hadn't gone in for *The X Factor* I would still be at college. Instead I'm traveling around the country – and other parts of the world – with four of my best friends, having the best time it's possible to have.

MOVING ON UP

I can remember so much about my *X Factor* audition and Bootcamp, but at the same time it all seems like such a blur. The best moment for me out of the whole thing was when we were told we were going to be put in a band together. I'd spoken to Louis, Zayn and Niall at Bootcamp and I remember thinking, "This is going to be a lot of fun," but I never for a moment thought that things would end up like this.

After the show everyone ended up coming to stay at my stepdad's house in Cheshire, and for the first few days or so we just bonded with each other. It was a new experience for us all because it was like living in a student flat. My mom and Robin completely left us to our own devices. We all put in some money and my mom put a load of food in the fridge and we were left to get on with it. I cooked dinner for us one night – chicken breasts, fries and peas – and we all sat around the table in the bungalow talking rubbish. Other than that I think we ate

Super Noodles most days, and we'd go out into the garden and play soccer for ages. We'd do ten minutes of singing practice, then play soccer for three hours, have a swim, drive to KFC … We were just messing around, but it was a really good way of getting to know each other's personalities. We were learning little bits about each other by having silly banter.

I got on with Louis from the word go. We're very similar and I like the fact that he has this ability to be nice to everyone while living totally for the moment. It puts a smile on your face when you see someone like that. I feel I can tell him anything, and I felt like that straight away. He can be really funny one minute, but if someone has a problem he can go into serious mode straight away and he gives really good advice.

Spain was so, so weird because we were still getting to know each other and then all of a sudden we were getting on a plane together for what felt like a holiday. We were still finding out so much about each other – in fact, we still are – so it was another really good time. I think we suddenly felt really grown up because we were in this big competition and, even though the X Factor staff were there, we were looking after ourselves to a certain extent.

Getting told we were through to the live finals was another moment I'll never, ever forget. We honestly had no idea whether Simon would pick us or not, so to get a yes was just the most amazing feeling in the world. We were in shock when we were phoning our parents to tell them, but we had to keep it quiet from everyone else, which made things a bit weird. I wanted to tell the world, I was so happy.

We went back home for a while after Spain, and with some money I borrowed from my mom I ordered loads of clothes for the live shows because I wanted to be prepared. I have paid her back now, by the way.

What was weird then was getting used to people knowing who I was. My audition was shown the day before I moved into the house, so all my friends were texting me to say well done. When I headed up to London we stopped at a petrol station and someone there recognized me, and that was so strange.

Moving into the house was cool, and I didn't even mind that our room was tiny. It did get pretty grotty, because you can imagine what it's like with five teenage boys sharing a small space. We had a lot of luggage and there was too much stuff in the room, so it ended up being a bit grim. Apparently at one point someone took a swab from the wall and sent it off to a lab for testing and it had loads of different types of bacteria on it.

We did try to keep the room tidy, but the longer we were in the show the more stuff we accumulated, and the room seemed to get smaller and smaller. I can't have disliked it that much, though, because Louis and I are planning to move in together. It must have been bearable.

I have so many great memories of being in the house, especially all of the times I went naked. Stripping off is very liberating, I feel so free. It's always a spur of the moment thing, but no one seemed to mind. I think Mary secretly liked it … I'd become a lot more confident during my time in the show through being in front of so many people, and my confidence came out in my nakedness. I also used to moon a bit at school, because it made me laugh, so I was carrying it on.

Sometimes I was totally starkers, and sometimes I wore a thong. My friend Nick bought me a gold snake-print thong for my birthday, and I took it into the house with me because I thought it would be funny, and then I started wearing it.

One time I had to do a naked video clip for ITV2 where I was standing there with no clothes on and the boys had to pass various objects across me, keeping certain parts covered. That was the plan, but at one point Zayn didn't move the

—

GETTING TOLD WE WERE THROUGH TO THE LIVE FINALS IS A MOMENT I'LL NEVER FORGET

—

STRIPPING OFF IS VERY LIBERATING. I FEEL SO FREE!

book he was holding quickly enough and the cameraman got a bit of an eyeful. I think you could safely say I'm not shy.

Performance-wise, I really enjoyed doing "Something About the Way You Look Tonight," which I suggested as soon as we heard about the Elton John week. I love that song, and I think it worked really well. We met some amazing celebrities as well. Simon Cowell and Cheryl Cole are absolute legends, and Jonathan Ross had us all laughing. Alan Carr and Russell Brand were really cool as well. I can't believe we got to meet so many of our heroes.

I found the *X Factor* final very emotional. We had no idea whether or not we would win, and when we came in third it really hit me. I cried as soon as we got off stage, and then I stopped, took some deep breaths and was fine again. After that, when we got invited up to Simon's office to discover our fate, I tried to stay as calm as possible, but on the inside I was terrified. As soon as Simon told us we had a record deal I started crying again and I sat there thinking, "Why am I crying? If this works out it's going to totally change my life." My life had already changed so much, but that was the moment that told me I didn't have to go back to doing what I did before. At least not for a while.

Even though I'd always wanted to be in a band and sing on stage when I was growing up, I never imagined it would actually happen. Imagine being told you could do exactly what you want to do for a job. It's one of those things you always want to hear, and then when you hear it you don't know how to react.

I couldn't wait to tell my family the news – in fact I wanted to shout it out to everyone – but of course we had to keep it quiet. I went back downstairs to the bar area because there was a little party going on down there, and I think my parents could tell from the look on my face what had happened. We all had a massive hug and all of us were unbelievably happy and excited.

A CHRISTMAS TO REMEMBER

I think we were all looking forward to having a break over Christmas. I missed the boys quite a lot, but at the same time it was great to just relax and see my family. Loads of my friends wanted to catch up, so things were quite busy, but I didn't want people to think that I'd changed and I didn't have time for them or whatever. Sometimes I'll be speaking to my friends for a while and they'll say, "It's so weird, you haven't changed at all," and that always makes me feel so relieved. Sometimes I stop myself from talking too much about stuff I've been doing, because even though it's my job I don't want to seem like I'm showing off or name-dropping.

I would hate anyone to think that I was trying to impress them. I don't need to; they're my oldest friends.

All of my friends have been so supportive of everything I've been doing. It was frustrating for me, because sometimes during the show I'd get a text and I'd want to reply straight away but I'd be whisked away – then everything would go out of my head, which meant I sometimes forgot to reply to people. But all of my friends were so good about it and so understanding when things suddenly became crazy busy. They knew that even if I didn't get to reply I liked the fact that they were still texting me and they were there for me. One of the great things about being on the tour was that we knew where we would be and when, so friends could come and visit us and we could catch up. It was much easier to organize seeing each other.

A lot of my friends are genuinely happy about how well things have gone so far and they like asking me questions. That's how I know who is a genuine friend and who isn't. I have come across some jealousy, and some people have made comments and distanced themselves from me without actually letting me know. I've tried to talk to them as I always would and they're a bit cold with me. When you've been close to someone it's hard when they start acting that way towards

ALL OF MY FRIENDS HAVE BEEN SO SUPPORTIVE OF EVERYTHING I'VE BEEN DOING

you. I'm not going to chase after people and beg them to be my friend, but I wouldn't want them to think I don't care, because I do. So while some people assume or think I've changed, it's actually them who have changed.

There are times when I would like to go home and just be normal and see my friends again and go to all of the old places. I enjoy spoiling my family, and there are times when I would love to treat my friends as well, and I know that my true friends won't think anything of it. I'm not just talking about money. It's also nice to be able to help people in other ways. For instance, my friend Ben is really talented musically and wanted to get some work experience, so I managed to get him some on the tour and he loved it. I would never have had the opportunity to do something like that before, but I'll help my friends out in any way that I can.

I'm trying my best to stay as down to earth as possible, so I don't want people doing things for me that I could do myself. Sometimes people think they should get me a bottle of water or some lunch, but I'm capable of picking up my own water, so why should they have to do it? It's nice that people offer, and I understand that if we're really busy and we don't have time to get lunch, or we're rehearsing on stage and we can't grab a drink, someone may get it for us, but if a bottle of water is in a fridge two feet away from me I can walk over and get it.

My mom would never let me get away with that sort of thing. If I was at home and I asked her to get me a drink she'd be like "You know where the glasses are." At the same time it's funny when I go home now because I'm so used to doing everything myself, but my mom still likes to look after me in a lot of ways, so I feel like a proper kid again when I'm back with my family.

A lot of people say nice things about the band and we get a lot of praise. Obviously it's lovely to hear and it always puts a smile on your face when someone tells you that you're good at what you do, but I want to keep my feet on

the ground as much as possible. I would never want to get big-headed. It's such an unattractive trait and I can't imagine myself ever being like that. I always want to be aware of staying true to myself.

I spent Christmas mainly at home with my family. That was the most important thing to me. That, and seeing my friends, which I managed to do a few times. Things had been so busy that all I wanted to do was have a break, watch TV and eat and sleep. I had such a nice time, doing the same family things we do every year.

One thing that was different was that some fans came to my house over Christmas, and it was so cold that I felt really bad about them being outside. I did go out and see them as much as possible if I was there, but I felt terrible that they were standing in the freezing cold because of me. As a band we've always said that we'll never complain about people coming to see us or wanting autographs or photos. They're the reason we're doing all of this.

We appreciate the support so much. It's great to know that people like what we're doing. Some days I read 100 great Twitter comments and there may be one from someone saying they don't like me. If I'm having a bad day for some reason, that's the one I remember and it can make me feel a bit down. Then I'll go back and read the nice messages again and they'll lift me. They mean a lot to all of us.

BACK TO THE FUTURE

The New Year meant getting back to work, and we knew it was going to be busy. We had the tour coming up, so we had rehearsals for that, and we also had quite a lot of meetings and gigs, so things were pretty nonstop. But we'd all had a good break and we were ready to get back into it.

One of the first things we did was go to LA. When we got told we were going there my mouth literally fell open. I love going abroad but I'd never been to LA and had always wanted to. I'd seen and read so much about it, so I was looking forward to seeing how much of it was true.

LA is something else. Everyone you see looks like they're famous, but I really liked it as a place. It was really hot there, so we were wearing shorts and t-shirts most of the time, and we got to chill out quite a bit as the hotel we stayed in, the W, had a pool.

What I found weird was that the people over there are so polite. When you get your breakfast brought to you in a hotel in England they'll drop it off and barely say a word, but over there they're so cheerful you want to invite them in to share it with you. This one woman who dropped off my food was like "Good morning, sir, how's your day going? Where do you want me to put this good stuff?" They literally couldn't do enough for you.

We did some recording in this really cool complex where there were loads of different things going on. In one studio they were recording the backing vocals for *Glee*, and then Randy Jackson's office was 100 meters away, so we went and met him and he was an amazing guy. He was so friendly.

We got some time off to go shopping too, so I literally raided Abercrombie & Fitch. Louis reckons I bought every single t-shirt they had in there, but I think he's exaggerating. I did get quite a few, though ...

I wish we'd had more time in LA, but we did really enjoy the five days we spent there. It was like I expected it to be, with the sun and the glamorous people, and it's definitely somewhere I'd like to go back to. I really want to go to Venice Beach and see what that's like.

We were all quite tired when we landed back in London, but we were soon woken up by the sight of hundreds of fans. It's become a bit of a legendary story now about us being mobbed and the police being called and everything. I'd never experienced anything like it in my life. We'd seen loads of fans at *The X Factor*, but usually they were either outside behind a gate or in the audience. And when we meet fans at hotels or outside gigs they're usually in small groups. Well this was definitely not a small group!

I was really shocked by the whole experience of having to run through the crowd, but I made myself enjoy it instead of being scared of it, because I knew it was something special. When we were in the police van afterwards we all sat there going "What the hell?" It was almost as if it hadn't happened, it was so surreal, but looking back on it now it was an amazing moment.

When tour rehearsals came around we were well aware that we would have to work really hard. We wanted to put on an amazing show and we had a lot of new stuff to learn, including dance routines. We were taught things like how to put more energy into moving around, which is hard when you're in an empty warehouse performing to no one.

We also had to practice putting talking bits in between songs, which also felt weird because we'd be talking to an audience of six crew members, and even they didn't respond.

Getting to put everything we'd learned into practice was the ultimate payoff for all the hard work we'd done. I can't even begin to describe what it was like when we all stood on the stage together for the first night of the tour in Birmingham. Looking out and seeing all the banners and hearing thousands of people shouting your name … It really doesn't get much better than that. We'd performed on *The X Factor* and we'd done gigs, but nothing compared to this. I had to stand there for a moment just to take it all in, but as soon as we started singing we were off.

I think even that first arena performance in Birmingham was different to anything else we'd ever done in terms of how much energy we put into it and how much we moved around the stage. It felt almost natural being there, even though it was also completely and utterly surreal. There were several times when we all looked at each other and I could tell we were all thinking the same thing – "This is incredible!"

The rush you get being on stage in front of so many people is indescribable. I wish everyone could have that feeling. I can be so tired and feeling like I'm in a bad mood, then I get on stage and I feel amazing. I'm so hyped up when I come off stage that I shout a lot and jump around. There's no feeling like it.

I loved the tour so much I never wanted it to stop. I didn't even get homesick, because we were so busy we didn't get time to think about it, but I actually felt really guilty about that. All in all we were pretty well behaved on the tour, but we had our moments, like the fruit fight. At least we didn't throw any TVs out of windows or anything … but there's still time.

The wrap party at the end of the tour was good, but we all felt sad saying goodbye to everyone. I was up until about five in the morning so I was a bit tired the next day, but we had a day off to chill out so it didn't matter too much.

When the tour was over, Louis, his mate Stan, my friend Johnny and I all went off on a skiing holiday together. I'd never been skiing before and I was desperate to give it a go. We had a brilliant laugh in Courchevel and I'd love to go back again.

We worked really hard on the album to find the right songs. They needed to be perfect. We wanted our first single to be a big summer song. For instance, when the Black Eyed Peas single "I Gotta Feeling" came out in 2009 it was the song of the summer. When everyone heard it, it reminded them of all the good times they'd had. We wanted our first single to be like that and be the song that everyone would remember.

The people we got to work with on the album were incredible. Steve Robson is very, very talented and has worked with James Morrison and Take That and all sorts of people. Working with RedOne and Rami was very cool too because they're legendary. It feels so odd to be working in all of these studios that we would never have even dreamed of walking into before we were in the band. It was quite surreal.

Having our first book, *Forever Young*, go to number one in the UK book charts was also pretty unbelievable. We were excited about it being out there and hoped that some fans would buy it, but we didn't realize just how many would get it. It was a complete shock and really exciting. The fans that came along to the book signings were incredible. I was given a lot of turtles because I once said I liked them, and it's so cool when people remember little things you've said and chat to you about them.

We've done so many brilliant things this year. Filming the documentary was an interesting experience, but we are used to the cameras now so we all felt pretty chilled out about it. Photo shoots are always cool too. Even though we've done them before, each time it feels like a new experience.

Going on the Alan Titchmarsh show was a good laugh, because it's one of those shows that everyone has seen. And he was a really nice guy. That was the first proper TV thing we did after *The X Factor*, so it's one that we'll always remember.

THE FANS THAT
CAME ALONG TO
THE BOOK SIGNINGS
WERE INCREDIBLE

LOOKING FORWARD

One of the surprising things about being in the band is how committed fans are to us. Some of them came to loads of dates on the tour. People still don't expect you to recognize them, though. There was a girl who was in our hotel one day who had been on loads of the tour, and she was really shocked that we'd remembered her name and knew who she was – but of course we do. We remember people just like anyone else would, and it's nice to have the chance to get to know them properly.

I'm not sure if I'll ever get used to the press attention. It still feels very strange when I pick up a newspaper and something has been written about me. It sometimes feels like I'm reading about someone else. But as long as people carry on writing nice things about us I don't mind.

As a band, we're having the absolute best time ever. We've become better friends than I could ever have imagined and it's so nice to have four other guys to share this experience with. If ever one of us is down the others pick him up, and we've got really good at coming up with ideas and putting things into practice as a group. I think we're going to get tighter and tighter as time goes on.

Out of all the things that we have coming up, what we're most excited about is getting out on the One Direction tour. We can see a lot more of the fans and they can see us performing our songs. It's down to us to show what we're all about, and we're looking forward to doing exactly that.

We've got a lot of big dreams. We want to have number ones, travel a lot, go back to America and have as much fun as possible. I don't think that's too much to ask.

QUICKFIRE

DOB: 2/1/1994

STAR SIGN: Aquarius

favorite ...

FILM: *Love Actually*, *The Notebook*, *Titanic* – there are so many (but I tell everyone it's *Fight Club*)

BODY PART: My hands, because I've always been told that they're soft

FOOD: I love sweetcorn

ALBUM: *21* by Adele

FRIEND: Louis Tomlinson

CELEBRITY LADY: Frankie Sandford

SHOP: Selfridges

DRINK: I've been trying to just drink water but I love apple juice

COLOR: Orange

TV SHOW: *Family Guy*

AFTERSHAVE: Blue by Chanel

PERFUME: Alien by Thierry Mugler

COMPUTER GAME: Fifa

IPHONE APP: Texts From Last Night, where people send in texts that people have sent them when they're drunk. My friend Ali and I send good ones to each other and some of them are so funny

WAY TO SPEND A SUNDAY: Asleep or chilling out

DATE VENUE: Restaurant

COUNTRY: England

RESTAURANT: TGI Fridays

WAY TO RELAX: I love getting massages because I've always had a really bad back

MODE OF TRANSPORT: Dog sleigh

NIGHT OUT: Going for dinner with all of my friends

BAND: The Beatles, Queen

WHAT COLOR IS YOUR DUVET COVER? Brown or pink and blue

WHAT KIND OF UNDERWEAR DO YOU WEAR? Boxer shorts. I like Calvin Klein

FIRST PET: A dog called Max

DO YOU LIKE YOUR OWN COMPANY OR OTHER PEOPLE'S? The company of people. I like being around friends and family

LAST BOOK YOU READ: *Forever Young* by One Direction

LAST FIVE THINGS YOU BOUGHT: A pair of shoes from Supra, an Adidas t-shirt from Selfridges, a Nandos, dinner at TGI Fridays and some toothpaste

WHAT TYPE OF GIRLS DO YOU LIKE? I don't have a type, because with some girls I may not find them attractive immediately, but then I really get to like them because their personality is so attractive. I like someone I can have a conversation with, and I would always look for someone who could get on with my parents. It's important to me that my family like her too.

LIAM PAYNE

KEEP ON RUNNING

I guess one of the strangest things I can tell you about my younger years is that I've only got one kidney because when I was born I was effectively dead. Weird, I know. The doctors couldn't get any reaction from me, so I had to be brought around, and although it seemed like I was okay, there were underlying problems.

I was born three weeks early and I kept being ill. From the age of zero to four I was always in the hospital having tests done but they couldn't find out what was wrong. In the end they discovered that one of my kidneys wasn't working properly, and because it hadn't been discovered in time it had scarred, and the other one was working at 95 percent of its capacity. It got to the stage when I had to have 32 injections in my arm in the morning and evening to try and make me better. I've still got both kidneys, but one doesn't work, so I have to be careful not to drink too much, even water, and I have to keep myself as healthy as possible.

DARE TO DREAM

My first ever school was an infant school in Wolverhampton called Collingwood and I was a bit of a naughty boy. In fact, I was often called into the headmistress's office in the first few days. I used to have water fights in the toilets and climb on the roof to get soccer balls back.

By the time I went to junior school I'd grown up a lot and I tried out for a lot of the school teams but I never got into any of them. Then one day I tried out for the cross-country running team and I came in first in the race.

There was a guy who was running for Wolverhampton at the time and he was one of the best runners around, and I beat him, so everyone said that I cheated. The next week we ran the same race and I won again, and that's how I found out I could run. From then on I was training all the time and getting up at six in the morning to run for miles. At the age of 12 they put me in the school's under 18s team, so I was running against 18-year-old men and keeping up with them.

I joined the Wolverhampton and Bilston running team, and for three of the five years I was the third best 1500 meters runner in my age group in the country, which was amazing.

I carried on being sporty in high school and I joined the basketball team, but some older kids picked on me because I had some really nice basketball clothes I'd bought in America. They decided that meant I thought a lot of myself, so they started bullying me. I was only 12 and they were a lot older, so I needed to find a way to defend myself. My sister had a boyfriend called Martin who used to box, so my parents suggested that I went along with him and learned to defend myself.

It wasn't the nicest gym in the world and you had to fight everyone regardless of age or size, so there I was, at 12 years old, fighting the 38-year-old trainer. I broke my nose, had a perforated eardrum and I was always coming home with a

OPPOSITE: **GETTING SOME EARLY BOXING PRACTICE IN!**

I USED TO HAVE WATER FIGHTS IN THE TOILETS AND CLIMB ON THE ROOF TO GET BALLS BACK

bruiscd, puffy face. But it gave me so much confidence. It was nerve-wracking at first, but I got pretty good over the next couple of years.

These older kids were still bullying me, to the point where once they chased me into the road. It all got too much so I stood up to them and ended up having a fight with one of them. Thankfully I won, but I nearly got kicked out of school for it, which obviously wasn't ideal.

I was a bit of a mini businessman when I was young. I really look up to the guys on *Dragons' Den* and I used to buy big boxes of sweets and sell them at school for a profit. I used to make about £50 a week and my dad was so proud of me. I never had any proper jobs because I was always busy doing singing gigs, so that's how I used to make my money.

I was always singing karaoke when I was growing up. I used to get up anywhere and sing Robbie Williams songs. I did my first rendition of "Let Me Entertain You" at a holiday camp when I was about six, and I didn't stop from then on. I've done karaoke in America, Spain, Portugal – you name it.

I always loved singing and dancing. My sister Ruth and I were always singing in the car, and my mom says that even when I was a really young kid I used to dance around the living room to Noddy. ! also used to put my dad's glasses on, clasp my hands behind my back and sing along to his Oasis CDs, pretending to be Liam Gallagher.

I've got two older sisters, Nicola and Ruth. I always got on really well with Ruth when we were growing up, but I guess because Nicola, being the eldest, was usually left in charge when my parents went out, I saw her as a figure of authority, so we used to bicker sometimes. Ruth and I are very alike in that we both like to sing and we don't really drink or anything, whereas Nicola is more of a party girl.

In Year Nine I joined the school choir and we used to do loads of shows in front of audiences, which I guess got me quite used to it. We set a world record when we joined with loads of other schools and sang the same song in unison. It was the Bill Withers track "Lean on Me" and it was great because I got one of the solo parts.

Apart from singing I liked science, and of course PE. My parents even suggested that I could go on to be a PE teacher. I was a big soccer fan and I used to play every lunchtime, rain or shine. I also used to go and watch West Bromwich Albion, and I remember running on to the pitch when we got promoted. It was a great moment.

Judging by photographs of me growing up, my hair has kind of come full circle. I had a big mushroom when I was a kid, then I had tramlines put in the side of my head and eyebrows like my sister's boyfriend Martin. After that I shaved it all off till grade three, then I grew it long again, so it's now similar to how it was when I was a kid. I keep thinking about shaving it all off again, because it would be so much easier to manage, but I'm a bit scared of doing it.

Clothes-wise I made a few mistakes here and there too. I used to wear this bright orange Umbro t-shirt and a special pair of shorts that I loved. I didn't really have much of an interest in fashion generally, so when my first *X Factor* audition came around I had absolutely nothing nice to wear. My shoes had a hole in them and I borrowed a pair of Armani jeans from Martin. He's a 34-inch waist and I'm a 28, so they were really belted in. I wore a large shirt and then I bought a £30 waistcoat, which was the only thing I spent money on. When I look back now I can't believe I got away with it. I did three rounds of *The X Factor* with a hole in my shoe.

Despite my hair mistakes, I think I got away with it at school. I had a girlfriend called Charnelle in Reception, who used to send me love letters. I was also really proud of the fact that I went out with a girl who was in Year Six when I was in Year Four. She was one of my sister's friends, and I thought I was really cool having an older girlfriend.

I'VE ALWAYS PREFERRED HAVING GIRLFRIENDS TO JUST SEEING PEOPLE

I really liked one girl called Emily and asked her out 22 times, but she always said no. Finally I sang to her and then she said she'd go out with me, but she dumped me the next day. My friends used to wind me up and pretend that girls liked me when they didn't, so I'd ask them out and they'd say no, which was mortifying.

I had a few dating disasters along the way, with girls cheating on me, and one girl was the inspiration for me singing "Cry Me a River" on *The X Factor*. That was my payback to her because she was unfaithful.

I've always preferred having girlfriends to just seeing people. I think it's nice to have someone special. I was seeing a girl called Shannon while I was on *The X Factor*. We were seeing each other for a while, but we had to be apart for months on end so it put a lot of pressure on the relationship and we finally split up. We still speak to each other, but it was just one of those things.

I was 14 when I first tried out for *The X Factor*. I had become really bored with running and although I was on the reserve list for the 2012 Olympics, I wanted to find something I could do apart from run. When I told my friends I was going in for *The X Factor* we had a bit of banter because they thought it was quite funny, but they were also supportive.

The only thing I really wanted to do was see Simon Cowell, and I waited nine hours in a line to get that chance, but it was definitely worth it. I felt quite grown-up at the time and like I was capable of handling everything that came with being on the show. But looking back now at all we've been through, there is no way I could have handled it. No way at all.

It was horrible to be turned away at Judges' Houses, but if I had made the live shows I wouldn't have known what had hit me. JLS and Alexandra Burke were in that year and I would have been gone straight away.

It was hard going back to school having done *The X Factor* because I got a real taste for performing on a big stage and all I wanted to do from that moment on was be a pop star. My schoolwork suffered quite a bit, to be honest, and I remember my head of year talking to me about my grades and things. I remember him saying, "Your grades are slipping. What if your voice breaks and you can't sing anymore? What will you do then? You won't have any qualifications to fall back on."

That really hit me and I started working a lot harder from then on and I ended up getting one A+ in PE, as well as two Bs, six Cs and a D. The school wanted me to carry on and do A-levels, but I went to music college instead. At least I did get decent grades in the end, though.

Going away for a few years after I first tried out for *The X Factor* and doing gigs was the best thing I could have done. I worked with producers and writers but I never signed any deals, just in case I ever wanted to try out for *The X Factor* again. If I hadn't made it I was going to do an apprenticeship with my dad, which seemed quite exciting to me, but first he wanted me to give the singing all I had.

My dad works in a factory building planes, and in my mind I was going to be playing with giant Lego or something, but it's actually really hard work. My other backup plan was to become a fireman. But then, when I was 16, I decided to give singing and *The X Factor* another go.

THE NEXT STEP

Trying out for *The X Factor* for a second time was really nerve-wracking because now I wanted it more than ever. Some friends and family members were even a bit worried about me going for it, in case I got let down again, but I knew I had

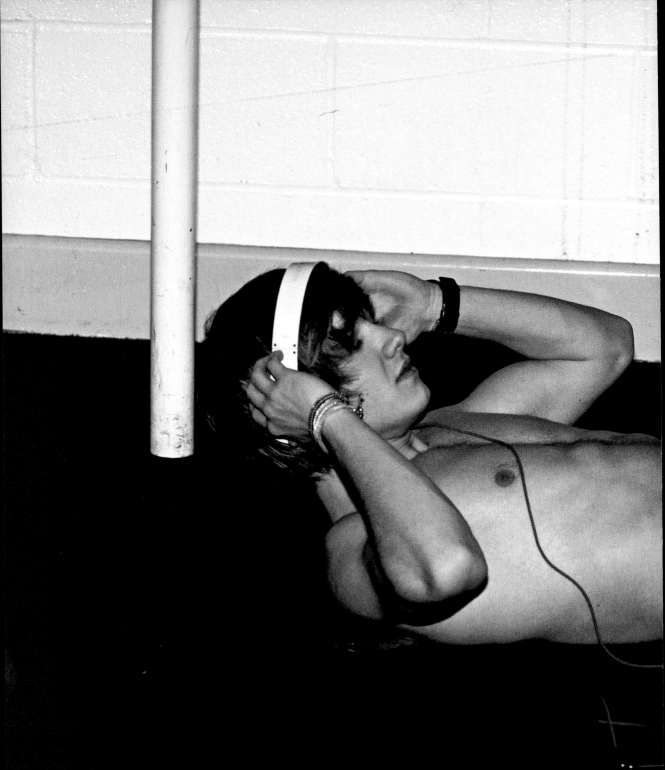

to try, whatever happened. I desperately wanted to get a yes from Simon and prove how far I'd come since the last time I was on the show. I'd grown up so much since I was last there.

Getting through to Bootcamp was just amazing, but then finding out I hadn't made it to Judges' Houses was crushing. I honestly thought that was the end of everything and I was so upset. So to get the second chance like we did left me virtually speechless. I was the only one of the guys who really had to think about whether or not it was a good idea to become a band. I'd been working as a solo artist for so long that I couldn't imagine not doing that, but as soon as I made the decision to go for it I knew I'd done the right thing.

I was quite nervous about going to Harry's stepdad's house, because obviously none of us guys knew each other, so to be thrown together like that and have to get to know each other so quickly was a bit scary. We're all quite different as well, so we did bicker occasionally. I had lots of friends at school, but they weren't all that outgoing, and Louis is so outgoing that at first I was a bit wary of him. He's a big influence on everyone in the band because he's the eldest and he has a sense of leadership, so he'll take charge of emails or phone calls from management. I'm more on the creative side, so I think we both want to take the lead in different ways, which meant it took us a bit longer to bond. We get on brilliantly now, though. As soon as we were honest with each other it worked, and we've ended up being really close friends.

We had such a laugh that week. We were all staying in a bungalow and we'd spend the days in the swimming pool or watching TV. We told ourselves that we were rehearsing, but we didn't really know what we were doing. We'd sit around and sing what we thought were harmonies and try out different songs, but really that week was more about us getting used to each other than anything else.

We've all changed so much since those days at Harry's house. We're growing up around each other in a way, and because I spend so much time with Niall I do an Irish accent these days without even noticing!

Going out to Judges' Houses in Spain was another big learning curve for us, because we got to know each other even better. We went out there to do our best and work as hard as we could to get through. Looking back, that week went so quickly and so much happened that I can barely remember everything we did, but I remember coming back feeling incredible.

We all went back home briefly before moving into the contestants' house. Then it was time to go again, and I remember my dad looking at me and saying, "Whatever you do, don't come back before Christmas." He wanted us to go all the way.

It was strange to be packing up and leaving home, knowing I could potentially be away for a few months or more. Also, a lot of the other contestants we were going to be sharing a house with were still strangers to us, which meant I was going to be working and living in very close quarters with people I didn't know.

Even sharing a room with the other guys was a bit of a shock. The room was tiny, and we spent all day together too. We all found little ways to have some time to ourselves, and that was very important. I used to get in and go straight to bed, but the other guys used to stay up a lot later, so I was always telling them off for waking me up. But I've honestly never met four harder-working guys. There was nothing we refused to do. Every time we were asked to do filming or interviews or anything we never said no, because we were determined.

It was good fun sharing the house with other people but, as I said, they were strangers, so it was a case of getting to know loads of new people. Apart from the other guys I got on best with Rebecca and Matt, and I still get on really well with them now.

I'VE HONESTLY NEVER MET FOUR HARDER-WORKING GUYS

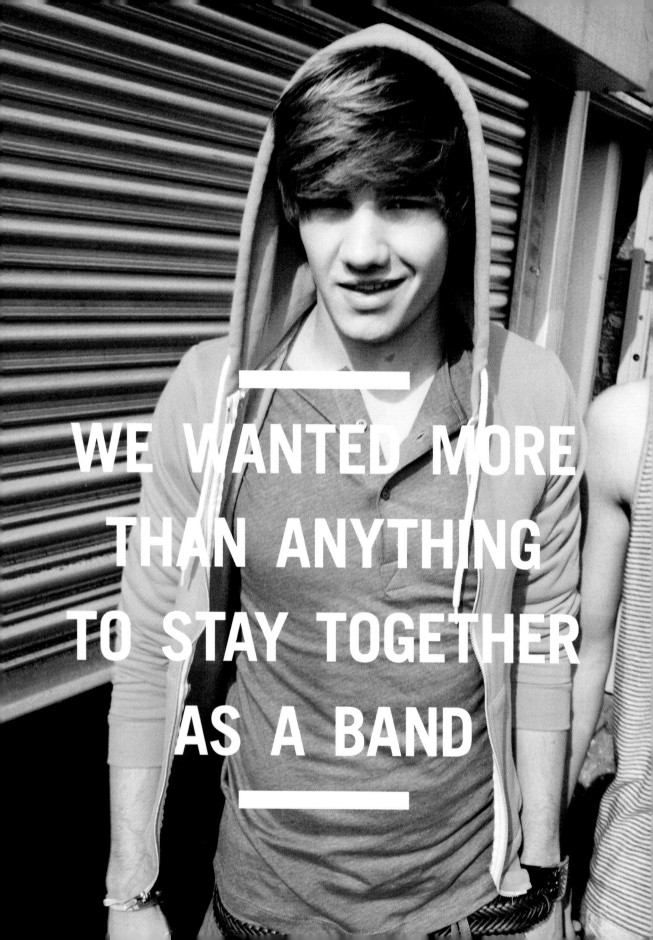

WE WANTED MORE
THAN ANYTHING
TO STAY TOGETHER
AS A BAND

For me, needless to say, the highlight of being on *The X Factor* was meeting Robbie Williams. He's one of the big reasons that I'm doing this now, so even just having my picture taken with him was amazing. I thanked him and told him that if it wasn't for him I probably wouldn't be in the show, and he seemed chuffed by that and was really humble about it. He admitted that he never knows what to say when people tell him they like him, because he's just doing his thing, but it meant a lot to him to hear it. He gave us great advice about staying down to earth, and he made so much sense.

Meeting Michael Bublé was brilliant as well. He was such a nice guy and as easy to talk to as anyone else you'd meet. It was such a buzz that he knew who we were as well. Imagine knowing Michael Bublé had watched you perform on the show!

Getting down to the final three in the show was amazing, but of course we were massively disappointed when we didn't win. We were completely happy with our performance of "Torn" though, so at least we'd done all we could.

We were standing on stage with Matt and Rebecca, and they called Matt's name out first. Then they called Rebecca's and we were so deflated. We hadn't experienced that situation before, because our name had always been called out on the right side when the votes came in. When I watched it back on TV it seemed like Dermot waited ages to read out Rebecca's name, but when I was there it felt like no time at all.

As soon as Dermot reads out Rebecca's name you can see all of our faces drop, and our fans in the audience kind of slumped. It wasn't that we believed the hype when people said we were going to win, but we couldn't help but hope.

Even when we were standing on the stage watching our best bits, knowing we hadn't got through, I couldn't help smiling. We'd had such an amazing time and

I kind of knew in the back of my mind that there was more to come. All the other guys were absolutely gutted, but I had a feeling that we'd be okay.

Seeing the video of all the things we'd done made me realize how far we'd come and how we'd made things work. We were thrown together and we worked so hard, doing a lot of things off our own bat, so even though we didn't win I felt so proud of us and I knew we were capable of going on to so much more.

I kept thinking back to those days in the bungalow right at the beginning of the competition, and it seemed like such a giant leap to be standing on that stage in the final. We hadn't even expected to get through Judges' Houses, so to make it all that way was amazing. At the end of the day I was deeply disappointed that we lost, but I was happy with how well we'd done overall.

Backstage afterwards there were a lot of tears, but even though I'd cried before when I didn't get through at Bootcamp, I didn't actually cry in that moment. I guess I didn't really know how I should feel. I'd been on a TV show for the past ten weeks, singing in front of 20 million people, and it was exactly what I'd always wanted to do. I felt like at least I'd got the chance to do it. But of course I was wondering whether we'd get a record deal, or whether this was the end of the road for us. I kept thinking about other people who hadn't won and who had done well anyway. Diana Vickers came fourth – and look at where she is now.

It was a tough situation, but we picked ourselves up as much as possible and waited to find out what was going to happen. We were then called up to Simon's dressing room, and we knew we were about to find out one way or another whether or not he wanted to carry on working with us. The atmosphere there was incredibly tense and we were all looking at each other really nervously. We wanted more than anything to stay together as a band and tour and record an album, but of course Simon made us wait a bit before he delivered the news.

It was like being back at Judges' Houses, because he was saying how much he liked us, but not giving us a definite answer. Then he told us that he was signing us and we were in complete shock. I had a feeling it might be good news, but until I actually heard him say the words I couldn't be sure and didn't believe it.

We went back downstairs afterwards and we were allowed to tell our families the news, but only them. It had to be kept quiet from everyone else, but needless to say it soon got leaked to the press. The whole night was full of mixed emotions really. And of course we were moving out of the contestants' house the following morning, which would be another big shift. We'd spent the last few months living in each other's pockets, so it was going to be very different not sharing a bedroom with the other guys anymore. We were all pleased to have our own space back, but I reckon all of us missed things about sharing the room in a strange way.

We moved into a hotel in West London straight from the contestants' house and we had the wrap party that evening which was a really good laugh. It was nice to catch up with everyone again and talk back over all the good times we'd had. We had to be up really early the next day for work, so we didn't go too mad and we were probably among the most well behaved.

The following few days were filled with management meetings and gigs, and while it was weird being away from the *X Factor* bubble, it was exciting to be experiencing new things. The reception we got in the clubs we went to was amazing, and we felt more like a band than ever because we were out there doing proper shows with a set list of songs. We could have happily carried on doing that for weeks, but then Christmas rolled around and I think we were all in need of a bit of a break after the madness of the recent months.

MERRY CHRISTMAS EVERYONE

Going home to my family for Christmas was really nice. Everything felt so relaxed and I felt closer to my parents than I've ever felt before. I could tell they were very proud of me, and I think because I'd been away it made the time we spent together much more special.

I think it was the same with the boys and me. We'd spent so much time together that we kind of needed a break from each other, and that made us all miss each other and appreciate everything we'd achieved. We did text sometimes, but we also gave each other space, so when we met up after Christmas we were so happy to be together again.

It was weird being at home and not having loads of things to do. I was so used to being busy 24 hours a day that sitting watching TV and relaxing felt completely alien. My sister Ruth and I ended up going to the cinema or bowling, because I needed something to do all the time. I couldn't just sit there and do nothing.

Christmas Day itself was lovely, with loads of great presents. I'm usually very cautious with money because of the businessman side of me, but this time I really splashed out – it was the first time I'd really been able to. I ended up buying four iPads, a laptop, a phone for my mom's birthday and lots of Links of London bracelets. I took the family out for dinner and really treated them, and I loved being able to do that. I also bought my mate some sneakers. Sometimes I'm not clever with money, because if I see something that will make someone happy I just want to buy it, but then there is the business side of me that tells me to be sensible.

My friends and family didn't treat me any differently because of the show, although I think my parents maybe treated me as more of a grown-up in a way. I think my mom found it a bit hard because I've always been the baby of the family and she knew I would be moving away in the new year. She's got no one to look after now, so she still likes to do my washing and even tries to pack my suitcase. But I do my own ironing.

IT ALL KICKS OFF AGAIN

It was weird to sit back and think about how different my life had become in a few short months. As everyone knows I'm a massive fan of Leona Lewis. I absolutely love her and think she's so gorgeous. Now she's added me on Twitter and says she can't wait to meet me. How crazy is that? Life is moving incredibly fast, and I do want to appreciate everything that's happening, so sometimes I just have to pause and take stock of things.

Straight after New Year's we were back to doing some more gigs, and we played at a few private parties. Then we heard we were going to LA for some meetings and to do some recording and we couldn't believe it. My dad always said to me that if we ever got told we were going to LA he wanted to be the first one to hear about it.

We had gone to have dinner with our manager, Richard Griffiths, at his house. We all left our phones in the car so we'd look professional, but when we sat down to eat and he started talking about us going to LA, my first reaction was to reach for my phone – I wanted to text my dad. I soon realized I didn't have it, so I was itching to get back to the car to let him know. He was so happy when he heard.

I'd never been to LA before, so I was looking forward to seeing what it was like, and it was so completely different from England. I can understand why all the stars go over there to record music, because it's the perfect setting with its

spectacular buildings and all that sunshine. We met Randy Jackson, who was amazing, and Bryan McFadden came over to say hello. Leona Lewis was going to come and meet us too, but sadly she couldn't make it.

We stayed in this massive hotel called the W, and we used to get up every morning and hang out by the pool. We were there to work but there was no set schedule, so it ended up being more like a guys' holiday at times. We went shopping and I bought loads of sneakers. No one bought as much as Louis, though, because he's got a shopping addiction. Zayn and I nearly made us late for our plane because we'd been taken out shopping and we got stuck in loads of traffic. We ended up rushing and panicking, but we just made it in time.

While we were in LA we went out to dinner with a massive producer called Max Martin and we did some recording with RedOne's crew. I remember thinking, "Wow, it's got to this."

The weirdest thing that happened in LA was finding fans waiting for us at the airport when we arrived, which we weren't expecting at all. They'd checked us out on YouTube and come along to see us, and they had a big banner and everything.

Our arrival home was the craziest thing I've ever experienced. There's only one way out of Heathrow, and it's the area where all of the celebs get papped. There was literally a wall of fans, so we had to go out of the main entrance and then slip out of a side door and run with hardly any security. I got hit in the face by mistake in the scuffle and some of the other guys had clothes ripped off.

When the police riot van arrived we had to run from this parking booth we were hiding in and try and get into the back of it, but someone had hold of my hood so I ended up being squashed up against the side of the van. In the end someone grabbed me and threw me into the back of the van. We drove off with

THE BEST THING
ABOUT THE TOUR IS
THAT WE GOT TO SEE
LOADS OF THE FANS,
WHICH I LOVED

lights flashing and siren sounding, so it was all quite dramatic. At that point we hadn't even released a song yet, so it was the maddest thing.

The best thing about the tour is that we got to see loads of the fans, which I loved. Everyone is always really nice and friendly. Sometimes we get shielded from it, but we would always rather go and meet them. If they're waiting at a gate at a gig we always want to go out and say hello, but sometimes the people looking after us don't think it's safe, so we can't, which is a shame.

We do have the best fans ever. I know all bands probably think that, but for instance Louis put on Twitter the other day that he wanted some Curiously Cinnamon cereal – and someone brought some to the hotel! It's amazing. It can be strange waking up to people screaming at 7 am, but we love it.

Even most guys are nice to us. I was in a restaurant the other day and these guys came over and they were chatting to me about the band and being really supportive. It's a shame when people aren't supportive, because at the end of the day we're just nice, ordinary guys, and we've come from nothing and worked really hard to be here. If they were in this position, they'd feel exactly the same way.

The funny thing about fame is that I don't think there's ever a moment where you actually stop and think, "I'm famous now." There are moments that you have on stage or in the studio that are amazing, but it never really hits home. I remember being on stage in Birmingham and the lights were on the audience and I was looking out at them thinking, "This is my job. I don't care what it takes, I'm not going to stop doing this." Equally, when I'm in the studio I'll find myself standing there smiling at nothing – just because I'm so happy to be there.

We did our tour rehearsals at a place called Light Structures. It was quite challenging as we had to learn dance routines and everything. I'd done some dancing when I was younger, but we were learning so many new things. We were even told to try and walk a little sexily and I think we all found that quite embarrassing at first.

Zayn's dancing has actually got really good and he dances around all the time now. He's much more confident. We're five guys, and guys don't usually dance that much, so we've made sure we don't take the mickey out of each other when we're trying new things. We're willing to give anything a go and I think that's a good attitude to have in this industry. Also, with five guys together there's always a little bit of competition – even when we're just playing Pokemon against each other, which we do a lot. But I think that's healthy as it means we're all striving to be the best we can be.

We started off the tour in Birmingham, which was nice as it's now my home town. The first night was phenomenal and took us completely by surprise. Obviously when we'd done the rehearsals and come out of the elevator – the elevator which brings you up from underneath the stage – there had been no one there watching. Nothing could have prepared us for what faced us on that first night. We were waiting to go on stage and had our earpieces in, so we could hear some screams but not very clearly. We weren't expecting anything mega, and then we popped out of the elevator and we could see all the banners and One Direction t-shirts and people screaming. When you look out into the audience and someone's got your name on a banner, it doesn't really sink in that it's yours. I don't know how Harry feels, because the number of girls wearing "I Love Harry Styles" t-shirts is unbelievable. They love him.

We didn't have any pre-stage rituals as such; we just used to mess around a lot. On *The X Factor* we used to do a team huddle and talk just before a performance, but this was more laid-back because I think we had a better idea about what we were doing every night.

We shared a room with all the other male performers, and whenever anyone else was with us they'd mess around too. I think that's the thing with us – we bring out the silly side in everyone. We get away with a lot because the people who are supposed to tell us off are generally having fun with us.

The only time we got told off was when we had a fruit fight a couple of times. Louis is a spur-of-the-moment guy, and one night he started throwing fruit at people, everyone joined in and before I knew it we were all lobbing them at the walls.

We do have proper guys' humor. A couple of times right before we were going on stage Louis and Zayn would have competitions to see who could give each other the worst dead arm. We'd also play the word game where we were selected to say random words on stage. I had to say Rodney and Del Boy in the middle of a song one night. Someone else had to say combine harvester, and Ian Beale from *EastEnders* made it into a few tracks. Louis even did roly-polys on stage a couple of times. I think we were getting everything out of our system on that tour.

A habit of mine was to make sure all my clothes were prepared and that I was ready to go on stage at any time. This is because when I used to do gigs a few years ago my dad always drilled into me that I should always be professional. I've kept that with me, so even though we had a great time, we did take things seriously.

There were quite a few parties on tour, but I'm a fairly quiet person, so while most people went to the bar after the shows, I used to go to my room to be by myself. I've got a lot I want to achieve, so drinking doesn't interest me. I did go to the bar every so often and chat to everyone, but things were quite manic and we were performing to about 9,000 people a night, so time alone was good. After that level of noise, however, silence becomes an almost scary sound and

it's strange. It's something you have to get used to. When I'm on my own now I feel a lot more alone than I used to.

When I was living in Wolverhampton there wasn't a great deal to do, and the only time I ever went out was when my dad and I went to the local pub, the Great Western. It used to bore me sitting there doing nothing, and I'm still like that now. I'm just as happy to go somewhere and have a think, or go to the gym and work out, as be around people in a bar. Working out is really important to me, because it also takes out any stress.

I've already been described as the dad of the group, because I'm the one who doesn't drink. With only one working kidney I have to be careful with things like salt, protein and alcohol, so I guess that's led to me being seen as the sensible one. I think even when I am old enough to drink I won't. My plan is to learn to drive, so I can ferry the other guys around and act as security when we go out.

THE FANTASTIC FUTURE

We were all writing songs while we were on the tour, but it was quite hard because I didn't have a guitar at that time. I got it signed by loads of the *X Factor* contestants and then I gave it away to a friend, and I hadn't had a chance to get another one. We were constantly coming up with ideas for songs, because we all wanted to be involved in the process every step of the way. So there will be a massive sense of achievement and it will really be ours. We don't want to be one of those bands who just sing other people's words.

We were all really chuffed when we were told we could tell our story in a book, and we had such a good time working on it. It seemed no time at all before we got the call saying that *Forever Young* had gone to number one in the UK

hardback book charts, which was unbelievable. It was only when we went to the signings and saw how many people were there and how many people had bought the book that it all began to seem real. So many fans came along wearing really cool t-shirts and it was a great experience getting to meet so many of them.

I am clearly the clumsiest member of One Direction, though, and I kept doing things wrong. At one signing I drank a bottle of Coke too fast before putting it down on the table and it bubbled over and went all over my clothes. At another one I tripped up as I walked onto the stage in front of everyone. I'm a bit of a hazard.

During the tour I had a persistent problem with my trousers! When we perform "Forever Young" we have to jump around quite a bit, and my trousers kept ripping. One time they ripped really badly – from the belt line all the way down my leg. Another time we were waiting to come on for "My Life Would Suck" and Louis pushed me as a joke, and my trousers ripped all the way down again. I had to sing two songs with them gaping open because the rip was massive. There was no point in trying to disguise it, so I made a joke of it to the audience and everyone had a good giggle.

The wrap party was great – we felt both happy and relieved. Much as we loved the tour, we did around 60 shows, so we were all pleased to be having a bit of a break afterwards. The party took place in a nightclub below a hotel, and I only stayed for a little bit because I wanted to go and chill out. I think Harry and Louis stayed up latest out of all of us. Louis is definitely the biggest partier, but if you get us all in a room together we have a party every day.

I think me and the boys enjoyed the tour more than anyone else who was on it, and later this year we're going to be doing our own tour, which is probably what we're looking forward to more than anything. It's going to be more full-on than the X Factor tour, and we'll be able to come up with loads of ideas and have a lot of input. We'll also get to see all of the fans and do what we do best.

After the tour finished I took my mom and dad away on holiday to Florida, and they had a great time visiting Universal Studios. Whenever we'd been in the past we didn't have a lot of money, so we'd have to line up for ages for the rides. This time I decided to spoil us, and I bought VIP passes so we didn't have to wait longer than five minutes to get on anything. We went out for nice meals and it was great to spend time together. For me it was good to rest my head after the whole *X Factor* experience.

We've enjoyed every minute of the writing and recording for the album. It was nerve-wracking trying to find the first single, because of course we wanted it to be perfect. We worked with some amazing writers and producers and it felt incredible to have these people on our side. For me the most exciting person we've worked with so far is a guy called Claude Kelly, who wrote "Grenade" and "My Life Would Suck." He's like a hit machine. We all got to do a lot of co-writing on the album, which was really important for us and we loved being involved.

We had a trip to Sweden and another to LA, which were both amazing. We were in LA for three weeks, so we got to see loads more than the last time, but we had to keep our minds on the work. We still enjoyed it, because the work was actually a lot of fun. Every time we go away we get closer and closer, and there was plenty more bonding while we were there.

I do enjoy the traveling generally, but what I really don't enjoy is packing a suitcase. No matter how often we do it, I don't think I'll ever get over that feeling of having left something behind. Having to pack all of your clothes and things, knowing you're going to be away for weeks or months on end, is really stressful.

We're pretty much living in hotels most of the time at the moment, although we did share houses at times, which was funny but full-on! We're all going to get our own flats soon. Some of us are going to share – Louis with Harry and Niall with Zayn – but I think I'll get a place on my own as I quite like my own space. I love the boys to bits, but I know that when we come back from spending 24 hours a day with each other I'll want to have time on my own. I've always been like that.

We have worked a lot this year, and at one point I think we only had one day off in three months, which was quite mad. But everything is new and exciting, and doing shoots and going on TV shows is such a thrill that we just got on with it and had fun. And we've managed to pick up some good free clothes along the way.

I had a weird experience the other day when I was watching TV. I looked up and thought, "I recognize that bloke" – and it was me! We never got to see ourselves on *The X Factor*, so to see yourself messing around and knowing that other people are seeing it is just crazy.

We feel like we've already done some amazing things, and the album and tour are our main priority now. We're excited about making music that people love, and we've got a lot of great things planned.

My main aim for us in the long term is to be big in America. That's my ultimate dream. It's going to take a lot of work, but we're all really determined.

We don't have many days off but we don't mind. We all push each other and support each other. If someone is tired and we've got loads of work to do, we'll boost them up and we'll all pull together and make sure we get through it – even if we've only had two hours' sleep. This is our chance to have an amazing time doing what we love to do, and we're not going to let it pass us by for anything.

QUICKFIRE

DOB: 8/29/1993

STAR SIGN: Virgo

favorite ...

FILM: *Click*, and I love all of the *Toy Story* films

BODY PART: My arms

FOOD: Chocolate

ALBUM: *Echo* by Leona Lewis

FRIEND: Martin, Andy and Ronnie

CELEBRITY LADY: Leona Lewis

SHOP: All Saints

DRINK: Coca-Cola

COLOR: Purple

TV SHOW: *Friends* and *Everybody Loves Raymond*

AFTERSHAVE: One Million by Paco Rabanne

PERFUME: XXX

GAME: Pokemon

IPHONE APP: Flick Kick Soccer

WAY TO SPEND A SUNDAY: Staying in bed watching movies

DATE VENUE: Cinema

COUNTRY: America

RESTAURANT: Cosmo. It's a Chinese eat-all-you-can restaurant near my home and it's great

WAY TO RELAX: Massages, especially when I've got a bad back

MODE OF TRANSPORT: Car

NIGHT OUT: Bowling

BAND: One Republic

WHAT COLOR IS YOUR DUVET COVER? Blue

WHAT KIND OF UNDERWEAR DO YOU WEAR? Armani boxers, but that makes me sound very diva

FIRST PET: A terrapin called Frederick – I'm very inventive with my pet names

DO YOU LIKE YOUR OWN COMPANY OR OTHER PEOPLE'S? I like being on my own a lot

LAST BOOK YOU READ: *Forever Young* by One Direction

LAST FIVE THINGS YOU BOUGHT: A Greggs, some protein powder, a PSP, a hat and some sneakers

WHAT TYPE OF GIRLS DO YOU LIKE? I like girls who are quite quiet but friendly. Looks-wise, I love girls with curly hair, but apart from that I'm open to ideas!

LOUIS TOMLINSON

THE ROGUE

It won't come as much of a surprise to people to hear that I was always a very chatty kid and I liked to talk to anyone we met on the street. I went to nursery school in Doncaster, which was a lot of fun. I enjoyed being around other kids and playing games. I was obsessed with Power Rangers, and whenever I was asked what I wanted for Christmas or my birthday I always chose a new Power Rangers toy. The Red Ranger was my favorite. When I met Zayn I discovered that he was mad about them too, and we used to swap notes!

When I was four we moved to Poole, near Bournemouth, and it was lovely. What young kid wouldn't love living by the sea and being surrounded by amusements? I remember going on the Power Ranger rides on the seafront and being really excited. There was always a lot going on and it was a perfect place for a young kid to be. I went to a school there called Uplands for Reception and Year One. Both years I was there I won all my races on sports day.

After we'd been in Poole for about two years my mom got pregnant with my sister Charlotte. We then moved back to Doncaster and I started going to a primary school called Willow. I never did anything that creative there in terms of performing, but I was very confident and quite loud. Starting at a new school was quite hard for me, as I was only six, and I'd left my best friend Alex behind in Poole. I soon made friends again, but I was quite cheeky and used to get told off for it. I wasn't naughty as such, but I always liked to be the class clown and make people laugh. Luckily the teachers still seemed to like me. (In case any of them are reading this, I apologize for making that crazy assumption!)

In those early years I spent most of my time with my great nan Edna and great granddad Len because both of my parents used to work. My nan used to pick me up from school and take me to the park, and I was with her almost as much as I was at home. I used to have a great, great relationship with them, and every time I went around to her house my great granddad would make me an ice cream. I miss them dearly. My nan used to love *The X Factor*, so she would have loved seeing us on the show.

I feel very lucky that I've got quite a big family. I remember when my first sister Charlotte was born. I was about six and I burst into tears because I was so overwhelmed with the whole experience. I was incredibly happy, but I'd been an only child up until then so it was probably a shock to me. I've got four sisters now, Charlotte, aka "Lottie," Félicité, aka "Fizzy," and Daisy and Phoebe, who are twins. It's great having that many siblings, but I did always want a little brother. I'm not complaining, because all of my sisters are amazing, but I would have liked another boy in the house.

When I was growing up we didn't have a massive house and there were five women running around, so my dad and I had to stick together! I suppose in some ways it did teach me about women. I'm certainly not intimidated by them – because I'm so used to them. Having that many sisters has definitely helped

ABOVE: BIG THUMBS-UP ON SPORTS DAY
OPPOSITE: READING TO MY ELDEST SISTER, CHARLOTTE. LOVING THE HAIR!

me with children too, and people always comment how comfortable I am around kids. I absolutely love babies and kids, and the boys are always taking the mickey out of me for it. I definitely, definitely want kids of my own one day, so I can have that little boy I always wanted. So there is a slight possibility I could end up with around 15–20 kids if I don't have a son straight away – something to be aware of, I guess, for anyone thinking of marrying me (though I hope it wouldn't affect her decision).

Secondary school was a bit crazy for me, because I ended up switching schools twice. There were two schools in my local area, and the one I really wanted to go to was called Hayfield. I didn't get in, though, and ended up going to another school called Hall Cross. It was fine there but I never really settled, and although I made a couple of really good friends called Dan and Aiden, I just wasn't very happy. Then I got offered a place at Hayfield after all and I moved there. That was quite hard, because I was now 13 and everyone else had been there for quite a while and they knew each other. I was the new kid, so the first few weeks getting to know everyone were tough. Looking back I'm so glad I made the move because it was a great school and I had arguably some of the best times I've ever had there.

I went through a seriously dodgy clothes phase when I was about 13. I used to wear jeans and England shirts. I also adopted the fringe-over-to-one-side, spiky-on-top hairstyle that was popular around that time. I didn't take a massive interest in clothes until I was about 17 – in those days I just used to throw on jeans and a t-shirt – but now I'm totally addicted to buying them and I love shopping.

After about a year of being at Hayfield I got into a band called The Rogue. I was on a field trip in Norfolk and I was sharing a room with my friends Geoff, Jona and Jamie. They were all in a band with a guy called Stan, who is now my best friend. We all got really friendly and while we were heading home on the coach,

Geoff said they were looking for a singer and asked if I wanted to give it a go, which was weird really as they'd never heard me sing! We used to practice once a week even though we didn't have any gigs, and we used to play a lot of Green Day and think we were rock and roll!

At the end of every term we used to perform a song for our year group. One of the first songs we performed was "Mr. Brightside" by The Killers – which my friends came to associate with me for the rest of my school days. I really enjoyed performing and yet I never had the courage to do a whole school assembly because I was intimidated. So it's so weird to think that I've ended up performing on stage in front of thousands. After about a year and a half the band decided that they wanted to get a new singer, so Stan and I kept the name of The Rogue and started working with another guy called Ben, who is very talented musically. We used to do acoustic gigs, but it was more for fun than anything, and we never expected to make it big – I just loved the feeling of performing to an audience.

I had already done little bits of acting aside from school shows, as I'd had some TV work as an extra. Because my sisters Daisy and Phoebe are identical twins they used to do extra work as babies, and they got a role on a show called *Fat Friends*. My mom asked the director if I could be an extra, so I went along and that's where I met James Corden as he was in the program. He's a top bloke and now a good friend of mine. Ironically I was one of the first people ever to ask him for an autograph, and I've still got it at home somewhere. I'll have to dig it out and embarrass him.

After doing the extra work I started going along to an acting school in Barnsley and I got in with an acting agent. After that I did an ITV1 drama called *If I Had You*, and I had a small part in *Waterloo Road*. Acting is something I would definitely think about pursuing later on, but for now it's all about the band. I won't stop until we're absolutely massive.

I NEVER HAD THE COURAGE TO DO A WHOLE SCHOOL ASSEMBLY

Toys R Us was one of many jobs that I had when I was at school. We all had to do work experience at the end of Year 10 and, because my granddad knew the chairman of Barnsley Football Club, I went and worked as a coach there for two weeks and it was great. I actually wanted to be a soccer coach at one stage. Either that or an English or drama teacher, because I loved the idea of working with kids.

I also worked on the tills at Doncaster Rovers' Keepmoat Football Stadium selling snacks at half time, and the only thing I really liked about it was the free food. I then got a job at the Vue cinema, and that was great because I got to see all the new films. I was on three months' probation, but there were a few times when I called in sick and later they found out I'd been out at parties, so the three months turned into seven and a half months. I think they quite liked me and probably wanted to keep me on, but they wouldn't commit to giving me a full-time job. In the end it was actually *The X Factor* that ended that job for me. When I first applied for the show I had an audition on a day when I was supposed to be working, so I got a friend of mine called Laurence to cover for me. He forgot and didn't turn up – but it was my responsibility. It was the last straw and I got the boot.

I was also a waiter for a while. I wasn't the best waiter, but I used to get good tips because I loved a chat, and maybe a little flirting here and there …

I remember lots of stories from the parties I went to during sixth form, some of which were pretty crazy. One party, I'd had a few drinks and I missed my lift home and needed a place to stay so the obvious solution was to walk to the airport with my friends Rob and Curtis and sleep there. Can't say it's the best night's sleep I've ever had!

Just to make things more confusing school-wise, I failed my first year of A-levels at Hayfield – mainly because I'd been too busy having fun. I remember the day

I heard I'd failed. I was absolutely distraught, because I knew that Hayfield wouldn't let me back in to re-sit. All of my good friends had passed, and I knew that they would be going back the next year and then heading off to university and I'd be left behind.

I ended up going back to Hall Cross and starting A-levels all over again there. I had been studying Psychology, English Lit, PE and IT, but I later dropped English Lit because it was all a bit too much. It was a blow to me, but thankfully I was 17 and happy to make new friends. Even though I felt a bit of an idiot because I was a year older than everyone else, I soon felt like I fit in. Also I was the only one in my year who could drive, which was quite a nice position to be in as it meant I could ferry people around.

I passed my driving test first time. I didn't pass the theory test first time, because I didn't study for it, which wasn't very sensible, but I got through the second time, scoring 43 – right on the pass mark. It was great being able to drive everyone around in my 1.2 Clio. It had alloy wheels and central locking and it was my pride and joy. It was really my nan's car, but it kind of ended up being mine because she never used it.

One of the highlights of secondary school for me was when I landed the lead role in *Grease*. It was the first musical I'd ever auditioned for, and that was on the same day that I had an interview for a Christmas job at Toys R Us. My mom picked me up from my interview to make sure I went to the audition, because she knew I was in two minds about it. Luckily it went well and I was so happy when I was told I'd got the role of Danny. I still get emotional when I watch the video back, because it was such a special time for me. I felt so proud of landing the lead and I put everything into it. I just want to take this moment to thank everyone involved in that production. It was a fantastic part of my life and I will never forget it.

I was out all the time in that first year and had such a good time. That summer was the best I'd ever had. I went to France with Stan, then to Jersey to see Stacey, a girl I met on holiday, and to Leeds Festival, which was an incredible experience. I remember there were loads of house parties and garden parties. I also had a party myself when my parents went away, and that was phenomenal.

My whole family went away for two weeks, and they wouldn't let me stay at home, or even leave me the keys, because they thought I'd have a party. But I'd had a new key cut, and within an hour of them going away I was back in our house in Doncaster. I invited everyone on Facebook and Stan brought along a massive amp. We plugged iPods into it, and we had it on on full blast – with the patio doors open – so it was only a matter of time before the police came around and asked us to turn the music down.

I wanted my mom to find out about the party while she was still on holiday, to give her time to get over it, so I put the photos up on Facebook, where I knew she'd see them. Thankfully there was no damage and we cleared everything up, so it wasn't too bad and I didn't get into too much trouble.

When I turned 18 I started going out even more and I used to go to this indie bar called Priory. That got me into new types of music and I started listening to a lot more genres of music at home. The memories I have of that club are incredible; it used to be all I'd look forward to every week.

I am very lucky to have been blessed with a lot of very good friends; however for the last five years Stan has been my very best friend. The amount of hilarious memories we have had together is ridiculous but to name a few, screaming "Tony" at the top of our voices just because that was my neighbor's name, pretending we knew the words to all the "Indie" songs that come on in Priory and just singing gibberish, the time we said something mildly offensive to a woman we thought was French in France (it turned out however she was English) and of course the time Stan was so drunk he tried to take a wee in my sister's room. We have had so many funny memories together, not everyone has the pleasure of having a friend this close to them and for that I am very grateful.

I always got on well with girls at school and I had a couple of little relationships in Years Seven and Eight. Then towards the end of Year Eight I used to hang out at my friend Dan's house a lot and I got friendly with a friend of his called Arianna. I ended up seeing her for about eight months and she was my first proper girlfriend.

I won't lie, I was a bit of a flirt at school and I always liked girls' company. I really liked this girl called Beth, and we were friends for about six months, then we started seeing each other when I was about 15. We stayed together for two years and two months and we got on so well it was really nice. Later on it all started to get a bit too intense for that age, so we split up. After that I was single for a year and then I got together with Hannah, who I was with during the show.

All in all I didn't have loads of girlfriends, but I was generally with someone and I do like being in relationships. I wasn't one to play the field when I was younger, and I can't imagine being like that now.

TAKING CHANCES

In 2009 I applied for *The X Factor* but didn't get through the first round. For the rest of that year I had my heart set on auditioning again and at least getting through the first round. When I tried out the second time I was more driven than ever. There was a lot more pressure because I was desperate to get through. I didn't tell that many people I was going because it was more about proving

WHEN I TRIED OUT THE SECOND TIME I WAS MORE DRIVEN THAN EVER

to myself that I could do it. I lined up at two in the morning and there were already about 100 people there. I was with my mate Stan and we were literally in sleeping bags in the line. We kept napping and every now and again we'd end up being moved along.

The actual audition was absolutely terrifying, I sang "Elvis Ain't Dead" by Scouting for Girls and then "Hey There Delilah" by Plain White T's. It was such a relief when I finally got through. The thought of going to Bootcamp was amazing, especially as before that I'd only been to London a couple of times. Now I know it like the back of my hand!

The week before Bootcamp my granddad took me shopping to get some new clothes, and that's when I bought my first pair of Toms shoes – which, as many people seem to have noticed, I'm in love with! I probably own about 11 pairs in different colors now.

When I got to Bootcamp I could tell that some people were already trying to play the game, but I don't actually remember that many of the finalists apart from Zayn and Aiden, because I was friends with them. There was a massive hype about Cher even then, and even though I didn't speak to them much I remembered Harry and Liam well, because I saw them and thought, "You are definitely getting through." I had a photo taken with Harry because I knew he was going to be famous. I even gave him a hug and told him not to worry because I knew he'd be fine.

That was why I was so shocked when, after we'd been waiting for what seemed like ages, the last of the male soloists names were read out and neither Harry nor Liam were called. I was honestly more shocked about them not getting picked than me. After I did "Make You Feel My Love" at Bootcamp I didn't think I'd done enough to get through and I felt really upset. Dermot came over to speak to me off camera and gave me a hug, which was so nice as there

were a lot of people there and he didn't need to do that. I was still very worried about my performance and at that point I never expected in a million years to go through.

After we were put in the band Harry said straight away that his stepdad Robin had a place in Cheshire where we could hang out. It was so cool because we all stayed in this bungalow in the back garden and there was a swimming pool and loads of room to play soccer. I used to drive us around everywhere and it was like being on a freshers' week or something because we were all getting to know each other.

The bungalow itself was lovely and we had blow-up mattresses everywhere so people would just fall asleep wherever. Everyone got on pretty well and they're all great guys, but Harry and I bonded immediately and he's now my best mate in the band. He's such a cool guy and very laid-back and easy to talk to. I feel like I've known him for so much longer than I have. I guess we've got a bit of a bromance going on.

There was never a quiet moment in the bungalow and we talked about anything and everything, from past memories to the future. We used to make a campfire every night and Niall would play his guitar and we'd sing along. They were really good times. I think it is incredible how we'd met so recently and within a week we felt like best friends. It wasn't forced in any way, it just happened naturally.

Every song we did that week was sung in unison and we tried some terrible harmonies, which is funny looking back. We really didn't know what we were doing, but I think it was really important for us to have that time together before Judges' Houses. It would have been so hard to go to Spain as a five-piece band when we didn't even know each other and had barely performed together.

Going out to Marbella was another really good time for us. We all bonded even more and it was so nice being in the sun. We had fun, ate a lot of pizza and because Niall can speak really good Spanish, he could translate things for us.

Even though Simon Cowell is one of the most famous people you can meet I never felt starstruck by him, because he makes you feel so comfortable.

The low point for me during our time in Spain was when I got stung by a sea urchin. My foot swelled up incredibly, it was embarrassing to be seen hobbling along, and the first time I was shown on screen it looked absolutely massive. The timing wasn't exactly great.

Getting through to the live shows was an amazing feeling, and we were all on a massive high on the flight home. But we didn't celebrate or anything because we were sharing the flight with all of the people who didn't get through as well as those who did, and the last thing we wanted to do was rub people's faces in it when everyone had worked so hard.

We all got to go back home for a little while before we moved into the contestants' house, and my granddad took me shopping for clothes again so I had some new things to wear. I was so excited about seeing where we were going to be living because I knew it would be great, and it was.

We didn't get to spend as much time in the house as I'd have liked because we were so busy, but the time we did have there was such a laugh and we played a lot of table tennis.

Obviously there were times when things did get a bit much. When you've got five guys sharing one tiny room you can imagine what it's like. We had the smallest room in the house so sometimes when we were tired it could be a bit awkward. I did miss my own bed at times, and when things got really

manic I missed my old life and friends. But I would not change anything that's happened for the world.

I'm a complete mommy's boy and I have a really good relationship with my mom, but we were kept so busy I didn't get time to miss home that much. I did speak to my family a lot on the phone, and I got to see them every week on the show, so that made things a lot easier.

The first week of the show was something I'll never forget. What an experience! The whole thing was amazing. My favorite performance of all was "Torn," and it was brilliant meeting Robbie Williams. He's such a hero of mine – I'm a massive fan – and he lived up to all of my expectations. Michael Bublé is also a really nice guy, and being around Cheryl Cole wasn't a bad thing either. She was so lovely to us. I honestly can't think of one bad thing to say about the whole experience. And at the end of it, of course, we landed a record deal. Although we may not have won the competition, we still feel like we've done ourselves proud.

IT'S CHRIIIIIIISTMAS!

We only had about four or five days off for Christmas, but we didn't mind that because it was a really exciting time. I had a little bit of money to spend on presents for the family, and it was so nice that I could splash out a bit.

It's my birthday on Christmas Eve so we had some family around during the day and then I went to see my friends in the evening, but I didn't do anything too crazy. I was quite tired and I wanted to take the time off to relax.

The fact that I was better known now didn't make it feel any different from any other Christmas, although I guess I appreciated being at home more because

I'd been away for so long. As presents I got things like clothes, some money, a laptop bag and an iPod. I did well! But I still had to help clean up and do other things around the house, so nothing had changed.

We didn't talk endlessly about the show. I think my elder sisters found it weird that I'd been on the show and friends of theirs at school were asking for autographs, but I don't think the twins really understood it fully because they're still quite young.

Being back there brought home to me how much my life had changed in such a short space of time. I'm so lucky that I got into the band because I don't know how I would have managed to get through my A-levels. I didn't have the motivation to do them, but with the band I'm so motivated that I'm constantly working on stuff and thinking up ideas. I'm so passionate about it. I'd go as far as to say that I'm really organized with the band, and I've never been organized with anything in my life!

I kept in touch with the boys by text a lot over Christmas, and Harry and I spoke over the phone a few times. The guys also got in touch to say happy birthday, which was so nice. All of our families are friends now too, and my mom and Harry's have become really close. During the tour they even came to the Newcastle gig together for my mom's birthday.

When I got back to Doncaster I heard that a few guys I knew were talking about me behind my back and saying that I didn't deserve to be where I was. Certainly I've had a lot of luck to be in the place I am now, but at the end of the day I worked really, really hard, so regardless of whether or not they think I'm good enough, I am here for a reason.

A few fans came over to the house while I was home for Christmas, and people go to my granddad's house and knock on his door sometimes. I just feel bad if

I'm not there. One time some people waited eight hours for me, but I was out all day so I missed them, and I felt terrible.

I don't know if we'll ever get fully used to the attention from the fans. It's been happening for a while now so we are getting a bit more used to it, and we appreciate the support so much, but it's still easy to forget that people know who you are. Even if you pop out to the shop at 11:30 at night after a busy day you can find that people are taking pictures of you, and that's a very strange feeling.

Things I never used to think twice about doing I now have to give thought to. Even the simple things like going to buy toiletries. Mainly we just have to be a bit careful if we go somewhere that's busy, because things can be totally calm one minute, and then it can go a bit crazy.

I spent New Year's just going out with my friends and I had a really good laugh. Most of my friends don't treat me any differently from how they always have, and that's so important to me. They mean a lot to me and I would hate our friendships to change.

We all loved having some time off, but we knew we had a record deal so we were all excited about getting back to work and seeing what was around the corner.

NEW YEAR, NEW CHALLENGES

When we went back to work we knew we had a busy January ahead of us, and we were all ready for it. I'd had a really good rest, but I missed performing live and I was kind of itching to get back into it. Now we had some gigs coming up, so I was really looking forward to getting back out there and seeing all the fans.

I DON'T KNOW IF WE'LL EVER GET USED TO THE ATTENTION FROM THE FANS

January was also spent talking about plans for the future, and we were all set to start working on our album, so whenever we had a spare moment we were coming up with ideas about how we wanted it to sound and what kind of influences we wanted in there. We all knew that we wanted to be as involved in it as we could. That meant a lot of song writing, so we would bounce ideas off each other a lot.

When we were on *The X Factor* we absolutely loved being in the recording studio, so we were really excited about getting back in there. The studio is a great place to be because we get to hang out with each other, and we always get to order in good takeout. As anyone who knows us will know, we like our food. Then we heard that we were going to be heading to LA for work, which was a massive surprise, but a brilliant one. One of the first things I thought about, I admit, was how good the shopping would be over there. I love buying clothes, so I was already mentally planning what I would buy.

We went over for five days, of which we spent two traveling, so we were quite tired for some of it, but being in the sun made me feel much more energized and we made the most of the time we had. When we finally got to go shopping I was actually a bit disappointed. I bought a few things but I can get my Toms in England and that's the most important thing!

While we were there we went for dinner with a big producer called Max Martin, which was a bit daunting. He looked like a really normal guy with jeans and t-shirt, but we were still quite intimidated. We also recorded a track over there with RedOne's team and it feels very cool to say that we went to LA to record.

When we flew back from LA we had one of the best fan moments we've ever had. We had hundreds of fans waiting for us at the airport. We had to run through them all to try and get to our cars, but there was no chance of getting away. There's only one way out of the airport terminal and that's where everyone

was waiting, and as much as we wanted to see the fans it would have been crazy to try to go out there and sign autographs.

I got a real buzz from the madness of it all, but Niall was absolutely terrified. To me it felt like being on a rollercoaster or something, and I just went with it. When so much is happening and you don't know where to turn or where to go – and you know everyone is there for you – it feels amazing.

In the end we left through a side door, but everyone saw us and we were completely mobbed. I was wearing a hoodie and half of it got ripped off me. Later, when we went to a signing for the first One Direction book, *Forever Young*, there was a girl there who had brought the sleeve along with her to show me – and even asked me to sign it. I thought that was hilarious.

Rehearsals for the tour were another big thing for us early in the year. They were quite intense, and when we started practicing "Only Girl in the World" we realized that there was a lot more movement in it than there had been when we did the track in *The X Factor*. It wasn't that it was difficult, but there was a lot to take in and learn and we had to go over things about 20 times. We were all keen to move on and learn new songs, so we got a bit frustrated at times. We all gave everything a go, though, and you could see us getting better and better each day, and that spurred us on.

Looking back at how much we've grown, I definitely think all of the rehearsing paid off. When I watch our performances from *The X Factor*, anything that required a little bit of movement or energy – like "Only Girl in the World" – looks so different from how we perform it now. I think we've all learned to have a bit more stage presence and we're much more confident. Harry has always been the most comfortable on stage, but I think we've all caught up with him now. Going on *The X Factor* and playing in arenas so early on in your career is some of the best training you can ever have.

One of the best things about the tour was getting to hang out with everyone from the show. Matt is such a good guy and we had fun taking the mickey out of him, saying things like "Look at me, I'm Matt, I think I'm sick 'cause I won *The X Factor*." It was also great to be around Aiden again – he was always someone I could talk to outside the band.

Every night after the shows an area of the bar or a room would be hired for us to go and chill out in. I tended to go there every other night so I didn't get burned out. I think Niall was the only one of us who was down there every night – he loves to talk. He was always chatting away with the crew or the dancers. Even if we were down there he didn't sit with us; he'd search out new people to talk to.

Every now and again we'd get this urge to do some daft stuff. When we were in Sheffield we trashed the dressing room. It all started with me trying to throw an apple core into the bin and missing, which somehow turned into everyone picking up apples and throwing them at the wall as hard as they could. We were sharing a room with the other male artists and we all started picking up any fruit we could find, so there were oranges all over the floor and bits of pear all over the tables. For those five minutes it was so much fun. We knew we shouldn't be doing it, but we were caught up in the moment.

After the fruit fight I popped out to go to the toilet, and when I walked back into the room Vicky, the tour manager's assistant, had just come in and seen the mess. I acted dumb, saying, "What has gone on here? Vicky, I have no idea how this happened, I was out of the room. Let me help you pick all of this up." I started helping her but couldn't stop looking over at Zayn and smiling. Meanwhile Vicky kept thanking me, so I totally got away with it.

We did the same again in Liverpool, and this time we thought we would get away with it because we threw all the fruit into the shower and shut the curtains. We left the venue after the show and nothing had been said, then the tour manager

Cara confronted us with two pictures from the dressing room showing us the state of the shower. She looked at us and said, "What is this?" Zayn got all nervous. He couldn't look at her and just said, "I don't know, I don't know." In the end we denied all knowledge. I think she secretly found it quite funny.

During the tour we kept being given carrots. Basically, this was because in Week 2 of *The X Factor* all of us boys were asked what we like in a girl, and I thought it would be funny to say I like girls who like carrots. Ever since then fans have turned up to see us with carrot banners, t-shirts and loads of real carrots.

One night these two girls dressed as carrots were dancing at the bottom of the stage. A friend then gave me a carrot costume and I wore it on stage during a show. It was brilliant and I love all that. Mind you, I should probably be getting some kind of cut from farmers, because I'm sure carrot sales must have gone right up.

I loved the wrap party for the tour. It was a chance to kind of reflect on everything we'd done; in a way it was almost a relief it was over and to know that we had a bit of a break afterwards.

We had the most incredible time on the tour, but it was pretty hard work at the same time. We had quite a few nights out in the last week, and knowing that I didn't have to get up the day after the party was such a bonus. I didn't get to bed until 5 am, and then my mom drove me home to Doncaster, which took three hours. I was so relieved to get into my own bed.

I missed everyone after the tour had finished. In fact, I missed most things about it. People complain about the traveling, and it can get tiring at times, but we get to stay in nice places and see cool things so there's really nothing to moan about. I can't wait to do it all again – I can't wait to do our theater tour. We love seeing everyone and the feeling of being on stage is second to none.

During the tour we filmed the ad for the DS Pokemon game and we all got given one free, which was amazing for me, Liam and Zayn, as we're totally addicted to it. It was really cool filming it in a hotel room. We were just being really natural with each other and messing around, and it felt mad that we were filming a TV ad. That's big time.

The whole time we were on the *X Factor* tour we were getting more and more excited about the fact that later we were going to be doing a One Direction tour. It will be a good chance for us to show what we can do. We've been planning it all year and whenever we were together we'd be talking about different things we could try. We're excited about performing the album live for everyone.

After the tour finished Harry and I went skiing with our friends Stan and Johnny at Courchevel in France. It was really good fun. I'd never skied before, but by the end of it I was doing okay. We got recognized quite a lot but everyone was really nice and friendly.

When we found out that our first book, *Forever Young*, had got to number one we were so shocked. We got the chance to meet lots of the fans at the signings, which was brilliant. We couldn't believe the size of the crowds that came along, especially at a signing in Lakeside Shopping Center. With all the fans who had come to see us, and the shoppers who were there too, everywhere we looked there were massive crowds of people. It was so nice to be able to say thanks to everyone for supporting us.

Recording the album was a bit frustrating at times, because we were desperate to find the right single, but when it came along it was amazing. We've got some great songs on the album, which show off all our voices. We worked with some incredibly talented people, like Steve Robson and Wayne Hector. Steve has worked with Busted and James Morrison and loads of others, and Wayne wrote "Flying without Wings" for Westlife. In LA we worked with the amazing RedOne.

IT WAS SO NICE TO BE ABLE TO SAY THANKS TO EVERYONE FOR SUPPORTING US

WE'LL ALWAYS STOP FOR PICTURES IF WE CAN

He is someone we all look up to, so you can imagine how excited we were about that. We loved being back in LA, which we felt we knew a little bit already. We also enjoyed going to Sweden, where we thought the people were really cool.

This year we've been going on quite a lot of TV shows and also recording the documentary. We wanted to give the fans an insight into what life is like for us behind the scenes, and also give people who maybe aren't fans yet the chance to find out more about us. *The X Factor* was so full-on, with cameras on us all the time, that we don't even notice when they're around any more, so it will definitely be very revealing.

ONWARDS AND UPWARDS

I don't know if I'll ever get used to fame. We've got more used to situations like going into a hotel and there being people there waiting for us, but surprising things happen all the time and you never really know what to expect – that's what makes it exciting. The most surprising thing for me is how everyone thinks they know us really well because they watched us grow on the show and become who we are. Also, because people voted for us I think they sometimes think they've invested in us, and in a way I guess they have. People always say, "Can we have a picture of you? We voted for you so many times on the show and spent so much money." But we're happy to give them a picture whether they voted for us or not!

People always think the paps are really awful too, but everyone's been pretty good to us and we've got quite matey with some of them. We'll always stop for pictures if we can and if it's safe to do so. It's the same with the press. We're always happy to talk to them, although some funny things have been written about us. One newspaper said that Mary and Wagner were sick of us because we got Cher's teddies and put them around Wagner when he was asleep on tour.

Apparently we were terrorizing him! But it wasn't at all true, it was all really lighthearted. We have no idea how the papers get hold of the stories, but some of them are both ridiculous and brilliant.

My hopes for the future? To take over the world. Ideally we want a number one single and album, and I'd like to go to LA again and also get a nomination for a BRIT Award. You've got to aim high!

QUICKFIRE

DOB: 12/24/1991

STAR SIGN: Capricorn

favorite ...

BOOK: David Beckham's autobiography – or the half of it I read before my dog chewed it up (actual true story)

FILM: *Grease*

BODY PART: My mouth, because without it I wouldn't have a job!

FOOD: Pasta and pizza, and on the dessert front "Cookie Dough" from Pizza Hut

ALBUM: *21* by Adele and *How to Save a Life* by The Fray

FRIEND: Stan

CELEBRITY LADY: Cheryl Cole or Diana Vickers

SHOP: Topman

DRINK: "Daim Bar" milk shake

COLOR: Red

TV SHOW: *One Tree Hill* and *Skins*

AFTERSHAVE: I don't have one. I think if a guy smells really strongly of aftershave it seems like he's trying too hard

FAVORITE PERFUME: I don't have a particular one; I just like a girl to smell good

COMPUTER GAME: Fifa

IPHONE APP: Twitter

WAY TO SPEND A SUNDAY: In bed with some Curiously Cinnamon, then a bacon, fried egg and cheese sandwich with a bit of brown sauce to dip it into. I'd have a game of Fifa, invite Stan around, have a lazy day playing computer games and have a kick around at the park

DATE VENUE: Cinema (simple but effective)

COUNTRY: France

RESTAURANT: Pizza Hut, because of the Cookie Dough dessert

WAY TO RELAX: Being around friends

MODE OF TRANSPORT: Car

NIGHT OUT: A good house party

BAND: The Fray

WHAT COLOR IS YOUR DUVET COVER? Cream

WHAT KIND OF UNDERWEAR DO YOU WEAR? Boxer shorts in all colors

FIRST PET: A dog called Ted

DO YOU LIKE YOUR OWN COMPANY OR OTHER PEOPLE'S? The company of others. I'm a big fan of people

LAST BOOK YOU READ: I've only read the David Beckham book my dog ate. I'm not a big reader, whereas he devours them

LAST FIVE THINGS YOU BOUGHT: I had a spending spree in Topman and bought loads

WHAT TYPE OF GIRLS DO YOU LIKE? I don't have a specific look, but I like a girl who is spontaneous and bubbly and has a good sense of humor. And someone who is chatty like me.

NIALL HORAN

SMALL TOWN BOY

I grew up in a small town called Mullingar in the midlands of Ireland with a population of about 35,000 people. I lived on a street in the town center, and then when I was about four I moved to an estate farther out of town. I think my earliest ever memory is probably of going on holiday to New York to visit my auntie when I was about four. I also remember going up and down my street on a toy tractor – there weren't many other kids my age, so it was mostly me, my brother and his friends. I also remember the time I split my brother's head open with a table tennis paddle!

My parents split up when I was five and me and my brother went with our mom for a while. Then we lived between their houses for a couple of years. Then finally I ended up moving in with my dad, because he lived in town, so I had more friends there and it was more convenient for school and other stuff. I was always small for my age – and I probably still am – but thankfully I never got bullied at school because I tried to be friendly with everyone. I was always up for having a laugh and messing around, so I got on really well with most of the other kids.

ALL MY FAMILY REMEMBER THE FACT THAT I WAS ALWAYS SINGING SOMETHING OR OTHER

I absolutely hated my first day at school. My mom dropped me off and I started crying when she left because I didn't want to be there. I was only five and none of my friends were at the same school, so I was so scared of being all on my own. I soon settled in, though, and I began to love school. I liked it all the way through, right up until I left – apart from having to do homework, which I hated, and general studying, which I didn't do much of.

I was into music from a young age. We used to play the recorder at school, so I started that when I was about five or six, and from then on I got really into it. I always used to sing in the Christmas carol service in primary school, and my singing teacher, Mrs. Caulfield, said I should try out for the town choir when I was about eight.

All of my family remember the fact that I was always singing something or other. My auntie used to come over from America every summer and we'd go on holiday to Galway in the west of Ireland. Once when we were driving along I was singing Garth Brooks in the back of the car and she said she thought the radio was on. Exactly the same thing happened to Michael Bublé with his dad. Once he sang "White Christmas" in the back of the car, and that's how his dad discovered he could sing. He's my absolute hero so I like the fact that we have a similar story. My auntie said she always knew I'd be famous from then on, and she said it the entire time I was growing up, but I never thought anything of it.

I started playing guitar when I was about 12, and a year later I went in for a school talent show, singing The Script's "The Man Who Can't Be Moved." My mate Kieron accompanied me on guitar, and although it wasn't a competition or anything I got really good coverage in the local paper because they had someone at the show taking photos. That gave me a bit of confidence to do more, so after that I entered a small local competition, again with my mate Kieron, where I sang "With You" by Chris Brown. I won the show, which was amazing, and it made me think that maybe singing was something I was okay at.

OPPOSITE: **AN IMPROMPTU PERFORMANCE, DRESSED UP AS PO FROM THE TELETUBBIES**

I also supported Lloyd Daniels – who was on *The X Factor* in 2009 – in a small music venue called The Academy. I told him I was going in for it too, but he didn't seem that convinced about it. Later he came to watch one of the live shows and I bumped into him. He remembered me and said, "See, I told you to go for it." But he actually didn't!

In the November before I tried out for *The X Factor* I did a local *Stars in Their Eyes* show. I sang "I'm Yours" by Jason Mraz, which was a very lazy song choice, as Simon Cowell would say, and I had a great time. I did really well and got some good press again, and it was all useful practice for the future.

At school I was rubbish at math but I was good at French. We had a big playing field so I was always playing sports, and that took up a lot of my time. Although I wasn't necessarily academic I think I was intelligent, but the simple fact is that I spent too much time messing around. I thought school was all about having fun and acting like a fool.

I remember a geography lesson on my first day at secondary school. All my friends had been put in a different class so I felt like I was back at square one and I didn't know anyone. Then the guy behind me, Nicky, farted and I started laughing, and we became friends. (Ha ha – he's going to love that shout out!) From then on we were like best friends, and we used to sit at the back of the class singing traditional Irish songs, along with another mate, also called Niall, and the teachers used to be raging with us. We were always doing things to make each other laugh. I never got into serious trouble, though, apart from one time when we bunked off school for the day and I got caught. We all got properly told off for that!

I did okay in terms of grades all the way through school, and my teachers were always saying I had a lot of potential. But I was too busy messing around or playing soccer with my friends to really get down to work. One of my teachers told my mom that I was always in a world of my own when I was in class.

When I was about 11 or 12 I got a V shaved into the back of my head and left it longer on the sides. I was looking at photos when I went home recently and I have to say it looked disgusting on me! I think everyone has those embarrassing photos of mistakes they made when they were young, but some of mine were particularly bad. I would love to see all of the other guys' dodgy clothes and haircuts.

I was always into pop music when I was really young. I really liked Westlife and I used to go and see them in concert, so to get to meet them at *The X Factor* and have a chat was brilliant. They were such cool guys and exactly how I expected. They were just laid-back and down to earth. Must be an Irish thing!

I never really had girlfriends in the early days at school because I didn't see the point in being tied down at ten or whatever. I was always shy about that kind of thing in any case. I had my first kiss when I was 11, but I think I've blocked it out of my mind because it was so bad. I'm not sure it even counts as a kiss.

I had a girlfriend when I was about 13, but we didn't stay together for very long, and I've not really been out with many people since. I've still never had a serious girlfriend, but I would happily go out with someone if the right girl came along.

I've only got one sibling and that's my brother Greg, who's now 24 and works in a local shop near my home. We hated each other when we were growing up. I think of him in those days as the annoying older brother, and he thinks I was the annoying younger brother. I hated it whenever he even looked at me, and we used to fight all the time, which wasn't great as he was a lot older and bigger than me.

I used to try and be the big man and hang around with all of his friends, and he hated that. By the time I was about 13 he had left school and got a job. We had both grown up a lot, and that's when we really started to get along. Now we love each other and we're friends as well as brothers.

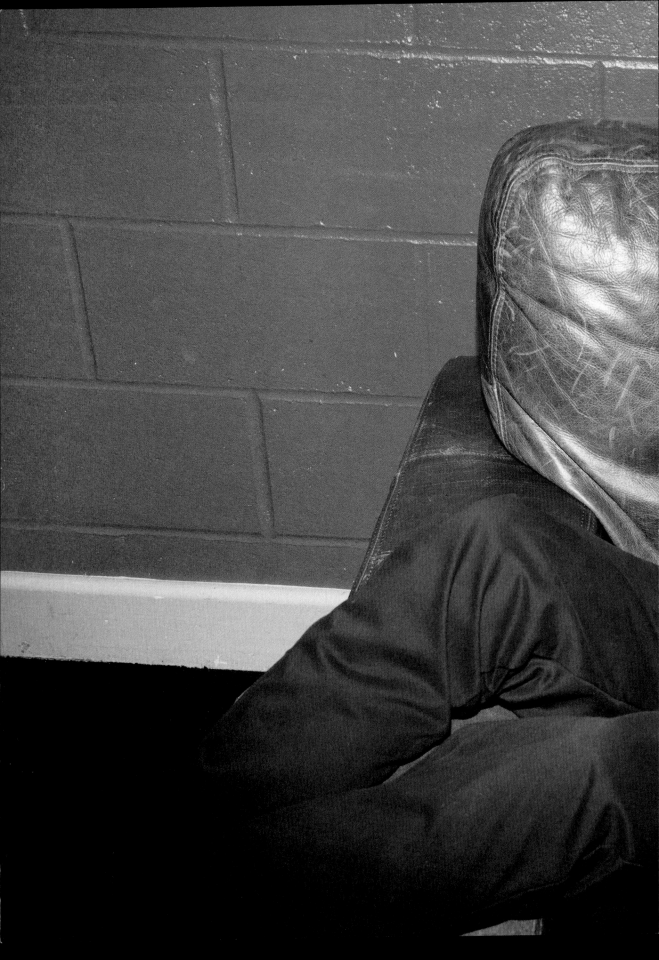

I USED TO TRY AND BE THE BIG MAN AND HANG AROUND WITH ALL HIS MATES, AND HE HATED IT

NEW BEGINNINGS

When I applied for *The X Factor* I was a student at St. Mary CBS and I'd just started my leaving certificate. The plan was to go to university and study sound engineering, but obviously that all changed once I got through to the live finals. At that point everything got put on hold, but not surprisingly I don't mind a bit.

I'd always known I wanted to give *The X Factor* a go – just like anyone else in the country who enjoys singing, I guess. My dream was to be an artist and be really respected for my music. I've been compared to Justin Bieber a few times, which I can't complain about.

It was summertime, we were in London in a hotel with 200 other people, and it was hilarious. And of course the highlight was at the end, with the five of us being put together in the band.

We were really excited, and we all took each other's numbers before heading home. We had decided that we needed to start practicing together and getting to know each other before we went to Judges' Houses; otherwise we would have been totally clueless.

We all agreed to meet up at Harry's stepdad's place, and we moved into the bungalow in the garden. It was pretty small for five of us, because there was only one bedroom, but it had just been refurbished, so it was lovely, and we slept either on sofas or blow-up mattresses. It was a great bonding time, and for me it's still one of the best experiences of being in the band so far, because that's where it all started for us. We used to play soccer in the garden and mess around. We kept telling ourselves that we'd get up the next day at nine and start rehearsing, but instead we'd get up at 12 and start watching TV. But that still worked well, because we had a chance to get used to each other before we started working together properly. In the end it all worked out naturally – we all just got on and instantly became great friends.

We had such a good time. We'd go to country pubs and have lunch and go and get ice cream from the local farm. We used to walk for miles as well; it was all very laid-back.

One night we were sitting around a fire in the garden when we heard this cry from the field. It was pitch black and we couldn't see a thing out there, but Liam all of a sudden turned into Superman. Zayn went into the bungalow and got a stick and wrapped a rag around it to make one of those fiery torches – it was like Braveheart! – and then they headed off to try and find the person who was shouting out to us. It wasn't until our hero had climbed over the fence and seen this great horse running towards him that we realized Liam wasn't as hard as we first thought! He came pounding back and jumped back over the fence as quickly as he could – we were all in stitches.

We did do some rehearsing, though, honestly. Liam and I both had our guitars and we'd take random songs like "Crawl" by Chris Brown, "She's the One" by Robbie Williams and "Fix You" by Coldplay and sing them together as well as we could with what limited group knowledge we had.

We really didn't have a clue what we were doing, so we basically headed out to Marbella hoping for the best but with no idea how we would do. Spain gave us more time to get to know each other and see what people are like in different situations. We took everything really seriously, but we also made sure we had fun. We wanted to make the most of it. We were probably the loudest band there – at any rate people were often telling us to be quiet!

On the day we were due to hear whether or not we were through to the live finals everyone was up really early for breakfast and the atmosphere was incredibly tense. We didn't find out our fate until late in the afternoon, and the boys and I spent all day talking through how we thought we'd done, while also trying to have a laugh to take our minds off things.

When we were first put together as a band Simon had told us that he'd given us a lifeline and he expected a lot in return, so not only were we doing this for ourselves, but we felt like we owed him something too. He'd given us another chance and we needed to prove to him that he'd made the right decision and we'd been a risk worth taking. (Hopefully we have so far!)

Standing there waiting for the verdict was one of the longest moments of my life. Hearing a "yes" would change things forever, and my mind kept going back to the performance – replaying it in my head and wondering if we could have done it better. It's so hard to read Simon's face, so it could have gone either way, and when he said he was putting us through I wanted to leap about ten feet in the air.

The first thing we did when we got through, apart from hugging each other, was to phone our parents. We were over the moon but we kept things quiet on the way home because everyone else was on the same plane, including all of the acts that didn't get through.

I flew to London and then on to Dublin. We'd been told we could tell our family we'd got through, but no one else. Somehow it was all over the internet so people kept asking me about it and I kept saying, "You'll just have to wait and watch the show."

I had about two or three weeks back home before we moved into the contestants' house, and it was strange packing up all my things and heading off, but I couldn't wait to get to London. As I didn't know how long we'd be away for, I took my whole life with me! My bedroom was literally empty when I left.

When we arrived in London we stayed in hotels for a couple of days while they finished getting the house ready. Then we moved in, and when I saw our room I wondered how we'd all fit in there. I'm very clean and I don't like a mess or

AS I DIDN'T KNOW
HOW LONG WE'D
BE AWAY FOR, I
TOOK MY WHOLE
LIFE WITH ME

my things being out of place, but Louis is the messiest person I've ever met. He'd just leave everything on the floor and I used to have to clean up after him. (Looking back, I do wonder why I did that!)

Our room was so bad that one day when we all went out for work, Esther from Belle Amie cleaned it for us because she found it so horrific. It was really clean when she finished, but it didn't stay like that for long.

Michael Bublé was without a doubt the best celebrity I met on the show. I am a massive fan, and I even made it on to his documentary, so I'll always have that as a reminder. He's an absolute genius, and when he heard that I was a massive fan he came over to me and introduced himself. I was freaking out. Sometimes people say it's a bad thing to meet your idols, but not in my case – he was so cool!

He was so normal and easy to chat with that I heard myself saying to him, "I spent £200 on tickets for your concert in Dublin and I had to give them up because of *The X Factor*." He replied, "Oh man, any time you want tickets for my show just let me know and I'll get them for you," but I turned around and said, "No Michael, I just want my £200 back." He started cracking up and then I got to go to his sound check, so I can't have offended him too much.

Katy Perry remembered me from my audition too, which was so nice. And throughout the competition we had a good laugh with Cheryl. Louis was always exchanging banter with Cheryl and she loved it. She could take the banter and give it back. She's so natural. She's like your normal girl from your area, but a hundred times more beautiful.

CHRISTMAS CRAZINESS

We moved out of the *X Factor* house the morning after the final and it was a strange atmosphere. Our room was such a mess and there was stuff absolutely everywhere, and we basically had to pack three months of clothes in an hour. There were some Mercedes vans waiting outside for us, and I was like "This is the life! I could get used to this."

We headed over to West London and checked into a hotel and then had a meeting with our management company to find out what was going to happen in the future. We heard some amazing plans and we couldn't wait to get started. That night we had the wrap party, and it was a great laugh, but we had to be up at 5 am the next morning so we didn't go too crazy.

We had a few gigs, and then four days before Christmas I headed home to see my family. And sleep a lot. I completely chilled out at home, but because I hadn't had time to do any Christmas shopping I had to go out and get all of that done beforehand. People kept stopping me in the street to say congratulations, and all over the place there were posters of me saying "Best of luck Niall" and "Good luck One Direction." It was so surreal.

It was a weird Christmas in a way. It almost didn't feel like Christmas because I felt like I'd missed the build-up through being so busy. On the day itself I was so tired I stayed in bed until 11 o'clock, which I never usually do. I'm always the first up. My friends and family didn't treat me any differently. I got the usual presents I always got from them, but I was grateful to be home, because it was all about to go a bit crazy.

I live with my dad in town because my parents are separated, so I went and had lunch at my mom's house in the country first. Then I went back home for a second dinner and all of my family came over. As it turned out this wasn't the best idea as it was so cold that all the pipes were frozen, so we couldn't even flush the toilet (ha ha, bad times!). In the end we had to move over to my cousin's house across the road and continue the party there.

The funny thing is that *The X Factor* brought my parents closer. My mom has remarried now and I get on really well with her husband Chris, but my dad didn't know him very well. Because they were talking all the time I was in the show and all traveling to London to see me, they started to get along really well. I remember my stepdad being in my house, putting the kettle on and chatting to my dad, and I was saying to my brother Greg, "Is this really happening?" In fact my dad and brother didn't always get on, but they too are now getting on much better, so the show has kind of brought everyone together. My dad and Matt's dad have also become good friends, and all of the band's parents text each other or chat on the phone. It's the 1D family!

I stayed in touch with all of the boys over Christmas, and I remember calling Louis up on his birthday on Christmas Eve. I was expecting him to be out partying, but it sounded fairly quiet around him. I think he was just so tired he wanted to chill out like the rest of us.

I went out with my friends for New Year and I did get recognized a lot, but I pretty much know everyone back home so no one bothered me in a bad way – they just wanted to chat.

BACK TO WORK WITH A BANG

After New Year's we played quite a few gigs, at places like Edinburgh, Leeds, Oxford, Hatfield, as well as lots of bar mitzvahs and a Sweet 16 gig. And, of course, we went to LA.

FOUR DAYS BEFORE CHRISTMAS I HEADED HOME TO SEE MY FAMILY AND SLEEP A LOT

Going over there was mad. They even let us go in the business lounge, and Liam, Harry and I had massages while Louis and Zayn played pool. The whole thing was just unbelievable. It was a very good start to the trip.

Loads of fans had turned up to see us, but they'd gone to Terminal 5 and we were leaving from Terminal 3, so we didn't get to see them which was annoying. But we did get to see rather a lot of them on the way back, which I'm sure you've heard about.

It was an 11-hour flight but I didn't sleep a wink because I was feeling quite hyper. I just watched loads of movies. We went straight to the hotel when we landed and checked in, then we went down to Jim Henson's studio. He was the creator of the Muppets, so there were Kermit the Frogs everywhere. The studio was like a massive log cabin.

We met up with RedOne, the production team who work with Lady GaGa and loads of other big artists, and they were just like normal guys. We also met Randy Jackson, and he was so cool. We even found that Cher was working there too. It was great to see her.

I'd been to New York and Boston before, but I'd never seen anything like LA. Everyone looks so slick – you feel like every person you pass is going to be a celebrity! Plus everyone is so chilled, which suits me down to the ground.

We did get some good work done while we were out there, but we also had time to go out for dinner and do some shopping. By this time us guys all knew each other so much better, so we felt really comfortable around each other and it was like being away with four of my best friends.

We were sad to leave LA but ready to come home, but we weren't prepared for what faced us when we landed at the airport. There were so many fans there and we only had Paul, our tour manager, with us. Airport security came to help us, but there were loads of paparazzi there as well so it was crazy. I'm really claustrophobic, so I was panicking a bit when we had to run through everyone and then hide in this parking booth. I was so relieved when the police riot van came and got us. I still can't believe that happened – it feels like it was all some kind of mad dream. It was really exhilarating.

We did our tour rehearsals in London and Wakefield. We rehearsed in London with a live band and also learned new dance moves and ways to move around the stage. We worked with a brilliant choreographer called Beth, and although it was a bit of a struggle for a few of us at first, I think we all did okay with that in the end. I didn't always get things right away, but once I got used to it all and got the hang of certain moves I did pretty much okay. Zayn's dancing has got loads better and he's really good. It's all about confidence, isn't it? And his confidence is constantly building.

Light Structures in Wakefield is a massive warehouse where they built the set we'd be using on tour, and there we went through the whole performance over and over without an audience. It was quite weird performing to no one, but it was brilliant for us because it got us used to how everything would look on the opening night. We also got a chance to get to know some of the crew we were going to be traveling with. Luckily they were all great and we had a good crack. I'm good with names so I got to know them all, and I hung out with a lot of them when we were actually on the tour. Shout out to the truck drivers! C'mon Fred and Bobby.

We arrived in Birmingham two days before the tour actually started, and we did a dress rehearsal. Then all of a sudden the first night rolled around, and I was petrified. There were 12,000 people in the arena and I'd never played to a crowd of more than 1,000 in my life. The whole place was packed and the pressure was on – this was our chance to prove ourselves. We were all really looking forward to it,

but really nervous at the same time. We wanted to put on a brilliant performance for the fans, because many of them would be seeing us for the first time.

In the end it went brilliantly. I was a bit shocked when I first saw the audience and all the lights, but then I couldn't stop smiling. None of us could. Afterwards it took us ages to calm down because we were on such a high.

Amazingly we didn't get into any proper trouble on tour, despite the now notorious fruit fights we had.

Food was a big part of the tour for us. The catering was so good, and every evening before we went to the bar or our rooms we'd go out and get takeout and bring it back, so we had a few good Chinese meals and lots of Nandos. Sometimes if we had a few hours off we would pop out and go shopping or get something to eat before the show. It was nice to be able to see different places. We saw a lot of different Nandos.

Of all the places we went to, Dublin was probably my favorite venue, and not just because I'm from near there. The crowd were just incredible. It was so loud, and when we came out of the arena I felt like I'd been on a plane for seven hours – my ears were popping. We did five shows in Dublin and each one was as loud as the next. My family came to see us there, they got really good seats and afterwards they came back to our hotel to chill out.

From Dublin we drove up to Belfast, where we had a really nice hotel and again the crowds were brilliant. To be fair, the crowds were brilliant everywhere we went. I couldn't believe how much support we had. Some of the banners were hilarious and we got to meet a lot of the fans. Quite a few of them checked into the same hotels as us, or they'd wait outside to talk to us, and although the security was tight we spent as much time as we could with them.

We were kept pretty busy. We got the odd bit of time off to shop or whatever, but we were doing quite a lot of press interviews or filming for TV shows or having meetings. It's unbelievable how hectic our lives have got in a short time. I knew it would be busy, but I'm not sure I ever imagined it would get this busy this quickly. We don't complain, though. We always just remind ourselves how lucky we are to be in this position. It's what we've always dreamed of doing, so it's worth every early morning or late night. We were literally having the time of our lives.

I went down to the bar most nights when we were on tour, but we weren't having wild parties; we were mainly just hanging out and talking. When you come off stage you're still buzzing, and I find it hard to go straight to bed, so that was my way of winding down after a show. Some of the other guys liked going to their rooms and watching TV, but they did also come down to the bar sometimes, and then we'd chat about the show and have a crack.

We spent a lot of time with all the other acts on the tour. There was a lot of pressure when we were on *The X Factor*, but on the tour everyone was so laid-back. It was a different kind of pressure, so we all chilled a lot more.

We had a good laugh on the tour bus as well. We had a few sing-alongs and messed around a lot. Most of the time on the tour bus we were basically either sleeping or singing.

Wagner was one of the absolute stars of the tour. He was constantly cracking jokes, even if he did sometimes tell the same jokes seven times a day. Paige was fairly quiet on the show, but on the tour he really opened up and was like a different person. He's really funny. I think everyone had the time of their lives.

We had a few parties in the run-up to the end of the tour, and the wrap party itself was good fun. A few people from our management and record label came

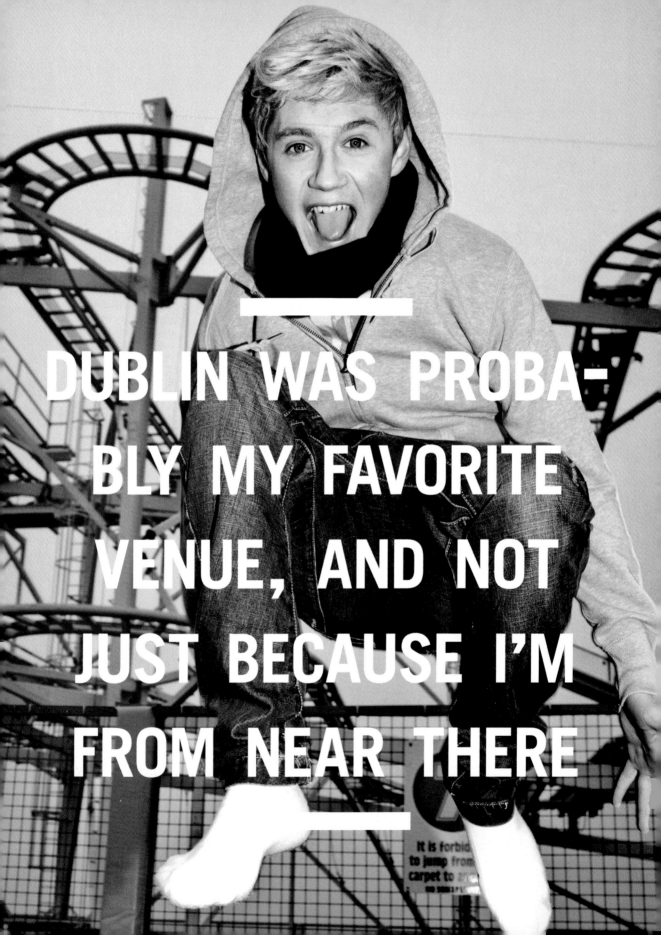

DUBLIN WAS PROBA-
BLY MY FAVORITE
VENUE, AND NOT
JUST BECAUSE I'M
FROM NEAR THERE

down, as well as our friends and family, so there was a good group of us. I stayed at the party until four in the morning, and I had to leave the hotel at five to get to the airport to fly home, so I didn't get any sleep at all. You can imagine how tired I was the next day.

It wasn't a crazy party. All we were doing was sitting around talking and saying how much we were going to miss each other. And we still do miss each other. We've stayed in touch with loads of people from the tour on BBM and Twitter, because we were a really tight group and we'll never have that particular experience again.

Afterwards I went on holiday to Spain with my dad and my best friend Sean. We know a few people out there and we met up with them, so it was a good laugh. Sean had his exams coming up and I decided he needed a break, so I paid for him to come and he loved it. It was great to spend all that time with my dad, too, because I didn't see much of him during the tour. We went to the beach a lot, and hung out by the pool, and we also found an Irish pub to eat in. It was great. Every time I go home I love to chill out with my family or just go out with my friends in town and stuff.

We had such a funny experience one day a few weeks after the tour. Zayn, Liam and I were all in Tesco somewhere – I can't even remember where it was because we were on our way somewhere in the car and just stopped off – and there was a guy in the line in front of us with a hat on like Matt Cardle's. We were joking about Matt being in the line and all of a sudden this guy turned around and it was him! It was so random. What are the chances of that happening?

After the tour we carried on working on the album, and getting to work with world-renowned producers who have worked with some of the best artists in the world was an amazing experience. Going to Sweden was incredible, and of course going to LA again was what we'd been waiting for. We had some meetings with some big people, and we carried on working on some of the songs we'd started on the first time we were there.

Our aim with the album was to re-create the boy band sound, do something no one else is doing at the moment, and of course enjoy the recording process. We didn't want to be sitting on stools and singing ballads. We wanted some big songs that would surprise people. The way the co-writing worked was that we would sit around and come up with ideas together. We wanted to be a part of the writing process, because of course you can walk into a studio and record a song, but you may not know what it's about. It makes a huge difference to be able to sing something that you've helped to create. We said from the word go that we wanted to be really involved, and we were very lucky that we got that chance.

Doing the book signings for the *Forever Young* book was unbelievable. So many people came along and it was so loud that I came out with a headache. There wasn't a single moment where it was quiet. The support the fans showed us was brilliant. I was given seven pairs of large plastic Shamrock glasses.

We love being able to go places and meet fans, and we also like doing press things like photo shoots and interviews. We've been on TV shows and all sorts, and the more we do, the more we feel like we're getting stronger as a band.

THE FUTURE'S BRIGHT

I didn't realize how many fans we had until we went on the tour. They were literally everywhere we went, and as soon as they found out where we were staying they would be there. Sometimes there were around 600 fans waiting outside for us when we left to go to the venue. When we were in Dublin they had

to close off the whole street, and all the fans were singing "Forever Young" at the tops of their voices outside. It was amazing. Harry was taking video of some of it, and we were equally amazed when we saw those scenes again. I've been to see bands like The Script and Westlife in Dublin, but I'd never seen anything like that before.

We have the most unbelievable fans. When we were staying in a hotel in Richmond girls were outside in sleeping bags or booking into rooms on the same floor as us. And every day after school there would be about 400 to 500 fans there. It's amazing how word spreads about where we are.

I honestly don't think any of us have changed yet and I don't think we will. If you ever spend a day with us you'll see that we're just normal guys who have a laugh. Obviously our everyday lives have changed, but I honestly can't see any of us ever getting big-headed or thinking we're special – there is too much banter between us for that to happen! We do have to be more careful about things like shopping, because even if we just pop out to get something and people recognize us it can go a bit crazy, so we do a lot of internet shopping now.

I'm still in shock about how quickly everything has happened. When we go on a radio show or we get asked for autographs we still have to pinch ourselves. And we're so excited about what's to come in the future. We've all got big ideas of what we want to do, and even when we were on the tour, and absolutely loving it, we were excited about getting back in the studio to start work on the album. That's because we were so desperate to get it out there, but we also know it's important not to rush it and to make sure we get it right. We want number ones! We also really want to go to the BRIT Awards – and hopefully be nominated for one next year.

We're excited about the documentary because that will show a different side to us again. At first it was funny having cameras around us like we did on *The X*

Factor, but soon we got so used to it that we didn't even notice them. So who knows what we're all going to reveal?

It's the same with the tour. We've got massive plans for that too, and we'll keep coming up with more ideas right up until the last minute. We want it to be the best show the fans have ever seen.

In 2012 I would like to carry on what we're doing and get bigger, better and stronger. I want to go everywhere and do everything! And we want you to come along with us all the way.

QUICKFIRE

DOB: 9/13/1993
STAR SIGN: Virgo

favorite ...
FILM: *Grease*, *The Godfather* and *Goodfellas*
BODY PART: My eyes
FOOD: Pizza, Nandos
ALBUM: *Crazy Love* by Michael Bublé
FRIEND: My friends Sean, Scott, Dillan and Brad
CELEBRITY LADY: Cheryl Cole
SHOP: Topman
DRINK: Water or Coca-Cola
COLOR: Blue
TV SHOW: *Two and a Half Men*
AFTERSHAVE: Armani Mania (it's the oldest of the Armani aftershaves out there, but I think it's the nicest)

PERFUME: Chanel Blue, Victoria's Secret

COMPUTER GAME: Fifa

IPHONE APP: Flick Kick Soccer, Sky Mobile

WAY TO SPEND A SUNDAY: Asleep for as long as possible

DATE VENUE: Nandos

COUNTRY: Ireland

RESTAURANT: Nandos

WAY TO RELAX: Sitting and playing the guitar

MODE OF TRANSPORT: Plane

NIGHT OUT: In Mulingar with my friends having a laugh

BAND: The Script, The Coronas, The Eagles, The Kooks, The Doors, Thin Lizzy, Take That and Westlife

WHAT COLOR IS YOUR DUVET COVER? White with a black pattern

WHAT KIND OF UNDERWEAR DO YOU WEAR? Boxers, Calvin Kleins (I'm wearing Simpsons ones today)

FIRST PET: Two goldfish called Tom and Jerry that my brother killed by feeding them too much

DO YOU LIKE YOUR OWN COMPANY OR OTHER PEOPLE'S? I like both. I like being around friends but I also need time to myself sometimes

LAST BOOK YOU READ: *Forever Young* by One Direction

LAST FIVE THINGS YOU BOUGHT: A pizza, jeans, water, a pair of sneakers and a Macbook Pro

WHAT TYPE OF GIRLS DO YOU LIKE? I like someone who can take a bit of banter, have a laugh, and who likes the same things as me – if you go out with me you have to want to come to a soccer match. I support Derby County and I always have. I like the natural look.

ZAYN MALIK

EARLY DAYS

I grew up in a really big family with five aunties and two uncles on my dad's side. They all got married and had kids, so I've got loads of cousins. I don't know the exact figure but it's definitely in the twenties. They're all my first cousins as well and we're close – they're like my brothers and sisters.

I've also got three sisters of my own and I was the only boy. There aren't many boys among my relatives – probably only about five or six of us in the entire family – so I've been brought up with a strong female influence. That definitely had an effect on my personality and I was much more sensitive when I was growing up because I was around women all the time. I also think as a result I understand women more than the average man does, to be honest. I was with my mom and sisters through their ups and downs, so there were times when I needed to just lock myself in my room to escape, and I can still pick up on things like that now.

I'm the second eldest in my family. First there was Doniya, then me, then Waliyha, and ten years after me came my youngest sister, Safaa. Waliyah is like

Megan from the TV show *Drake and Josh*. She's a very, very clever young girl, and if you ever cross her path, she'll outwit you.

I like to think I am a nice big brother. I look after my sisters but I am also quite firm and I tell them if they need to go and clean their rooms or whatever, and they listen to me. I think I am pretty good to them too. Whenever I have a bit of money I buy them presents, and I always look out for them.

My earliest ever memory is of going to a fair with my grandma and my mom when I was about three. Everything seemed so big, and I remember the bright lights and the thrill of going on the merry-go-round.

I was a bit of a handful when I was a kid because I was quite hyperactive. If I got the tiniest bit of sugar in me I'd be bouncing off the walls and jumping from one room to the next. Even in the house my mom used to have to put me in my stroller and make me stay there because I was so hyper all the time. I had endless energy. But at the same time I was quite reserved and if things bothered me I'd keep them bottled up. I think being the only boy I wanted to keep myself to myself, and I spent a lot of time on my own in my early years. I had my own bedroom so I'd play by myself. I was very independent and I still am in some ways.

I didn't go to nursery school because I was pretty close to my dad and he liked having me around, so my first school experience was Reception. The night before I started I didn't sleep at all and I was really excited about putting on my new school uniform.

All we used to do in Reception was mess around and play with sand. Otherwise all I can remember is the chairs in class being really low and sitting on the carpet for story time.

OPPOSITE: **I LOVED SINGING FROM AN EARLY AGE. HERE I AM, AGE FOUR, WITH A MICRO-PHONE AND TWO GUITARS, ALREADY DREAMING OF BEING A STAR**

I was always really good at English and reading even when I was really little. My reading age was about the same as an 18-year-old's from the time I was eight. My granddad was constantly making me read things because he was so proud of how good I was.

I ended up sitting my English GCSE a year early and got an A. I wanted to re-sit and get an A+, but they wouldn't let me. They made me do more math instead, which never made sense to me as I couldn't stand it. I did art all the way through school too, and I seemed to have some talent. My dad is an amazing artist, so I got that from him, and I still love painting and drawing now. I'm planning to do some new pictures so I can put them up on our website, so keep an eye out.

I didn't really have many friends at the primary school I first went to, because I was quite into doing my own thing. Then after a couple of years I moved to another school, and while I was there I met a guy called Sam. We got on brilliantly and he was my best friend until I left that school. I was always the kind of person who just had one good friend and I'm still quite like that now. Of course I'm close to all of the boys, but I've never been the kind of person who needs loads of people around them.

Even now it takes me a while to get to know people before I can be properly myself. I don't let a lot of people in. As much as I love meeting people, I like to get to know people properly before I think of them as real friends.

I almost felt like I didn't fit in when I was in my first two schools because I was the only mixed heritage kid in my class. My granddad Mohammed was born in Pakistan and my dad was born in England. My mom's dad was Irish and her mom was English, so I'm Irish/English/Asian, which is quite a mix.

My granddad is very fair-skinned with green eyes, and all that side of my family has got very light eyes.

After I'd been at my first upper school for a year my older sister and I moved to a different one because she didn't like the one we were at. Our new school was a lot more mixed, so I felt like I fitted in much better. Also, all of the girls wanted to know who this new kid was, and that's when I became cool.

I was about 12 or 13 and I started taking pride in my appearance. I even used to get up half an hour earlier than my sister so I could do my hair. My dad has cut my hair since I was five years old, so he used to help me with my hair as well. When I got a bit older I started doing it myself and got into fashion and girls. I guess that's when I became the person I am today, at least in terms of appearance and thinking I was cool, even if I wasn't.

I had a few dodgy haircuts over the years and I shaved my head a few times when I was younger, and also had slits in my eyebrows. I thought I was properly gangsta, being into R&B and rap, and I thought they made me look hard. I also went through a phase where I wore jogger bottoms and hoodies all the time. Again, I thought I looked great, but looking back probably not …

I was really into drama at school and I landed a role in *Grease* in my early teens. I was too short for the lead role, but they made new parts for me and this other guy, Aqib Khan, as the young T-Birds. Aqib is doing really well now – he played the lead part in the film *West Is West* – and I'm so happy for him. We were good friends at school and did a few plays together. I also appeared in *Arabian Nights* and played Bugsy in *Bugsy Malone*, which was a brilliant moment.

I absolutely loved being on stage and becoming somebody else. I found being a character really liberating and I used to get such an adrenaline rush from acting. Singing was kind of secondary for me at that time. I joined the choir because

ABOVE: **POPCORN AND A CAKE — THE PERFECT WAY TO CELEBRATE YOUR FOURTH BIRTHDAY!**
OPPOSITE: **ONE OF MY FIRST PHOTO SHOOTS**

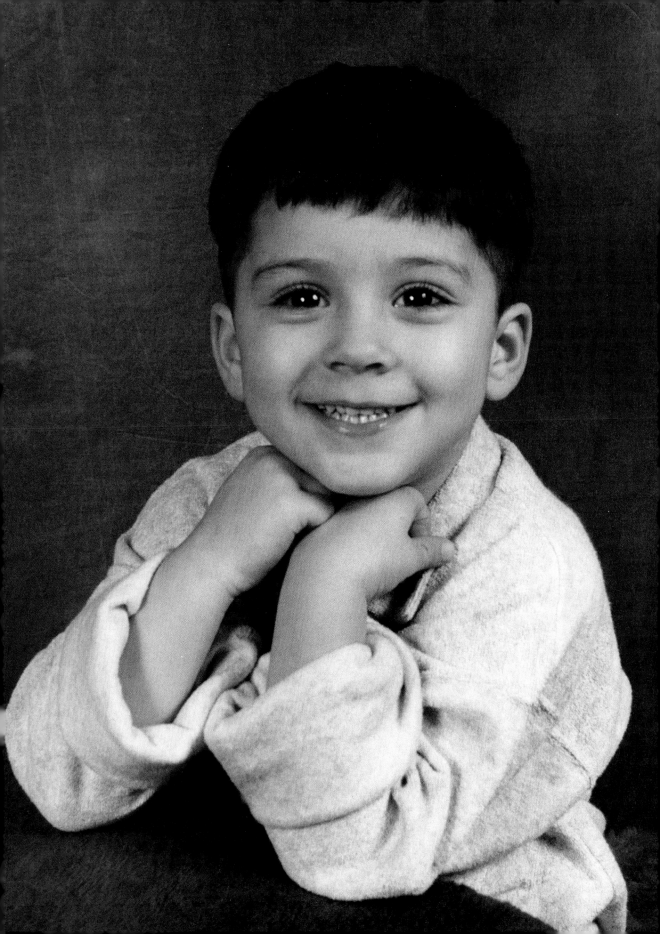

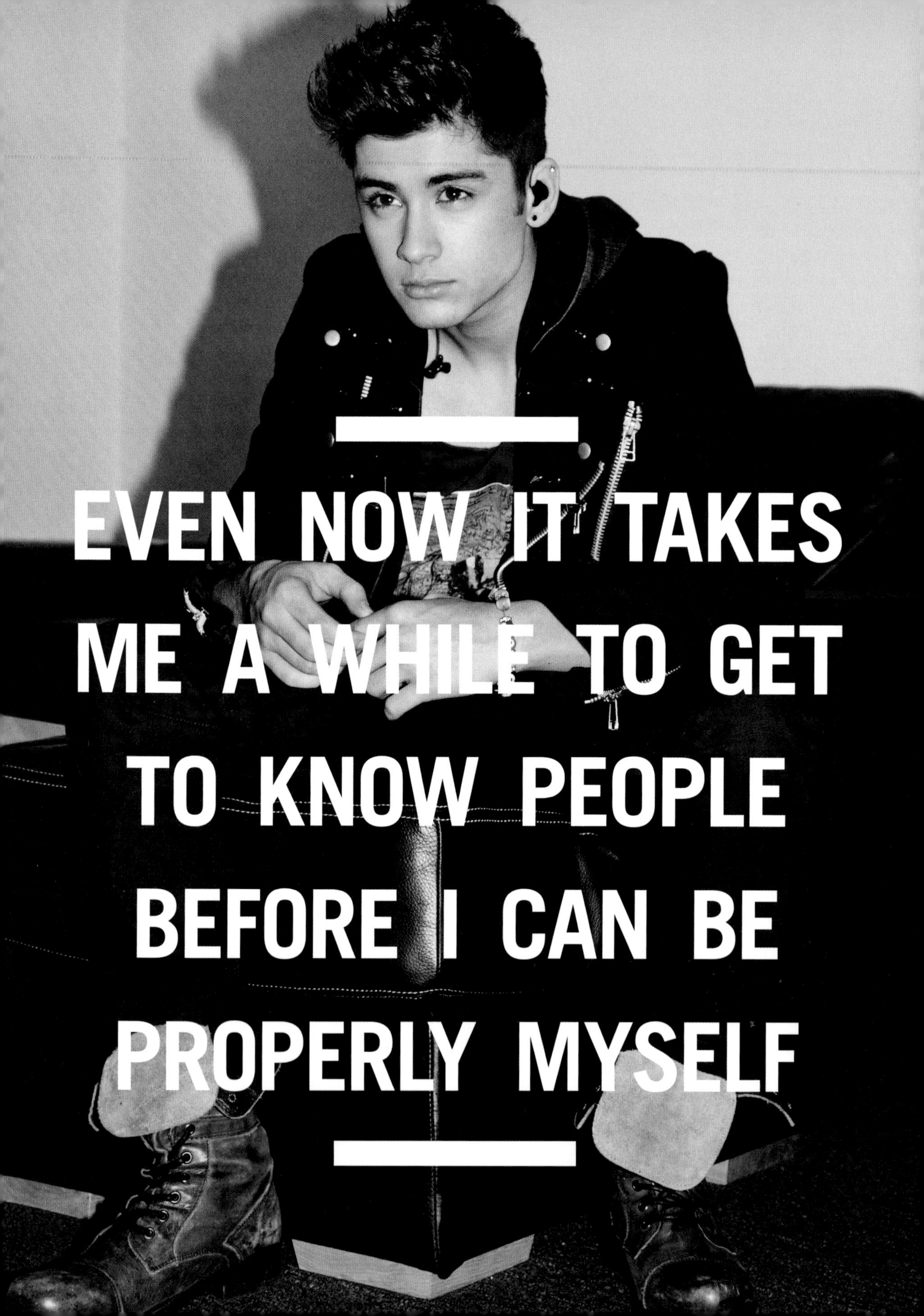

EVEN NOW IT TAKES
ME A WHILE TO GET
TO KNOW PEOPLE
BEFORE I CAN BE
PROPERLY MYSELF

the music teacher Mrs. Fox asked me to, so I was involved in music, but back then it was all about being on stage playing a character.

In my drama class there was a guy called Danny, we got on straight away and he too became a good friend. He was a year or two older than me, so through him I started hanging out with a lot of older kids. I also became friends with his brother Anthony, who is two years younger than me, and I started hanging out with the pair of them and going to the cinema and stuff all the time, and we became a little gang of three. They're still my two best friends now and we keep in touch all the time.

I was really short for my age up until I went to sixth form. All of a sudden in the summer holidays between school and sixth form I grew absolutely loads. I remember being hungry all of the time and having pains in my legs, and my mom didn't know what was wrong with me, but I guess they must have been growing pains. It was almost like I went to bed one night and woke up tall. Everyone was really shocked when they saw me after the holidays. Even a lot of the girls had been taller than me, and then all of a sudden I was taller than them, and I think a lot of people felt a bit confused.

I had my first kiss when I was about nine or ten years old. I was so short that I had to get a brick and put it up against a wall so I could stand on it and reach the girl's face. I remember thinking. "Eww, I just kissed a girl, that was horrible." It was only a peck, but I was paranoid that people would find out. I thought people would know just from looking at me that I'd kissed someone.

My real interest in girls started when I was about 12 or 13. Girls would come up and ask if I wanted to go out with their friend. I had my first real girlfriend at around 15, and I was with her for about nine months. I've only ever had two or three proper girlfriends.

I wouldn't say I've got a specific type when it comes to girls. I've become a lot less shallow as I've gotten older, and personality is very important to me now. Someone can be the best-looking person in the world, but if they're boring there's nothing worse. You have to have something to stimulate you mentally.

ONE GIANT LEAP

The whole *X Factor* experience was a weird one for me. At school I was never one to really put myself out there, but my music teacher suggested that I go for it. I first got the application form when I was 15, but I chickened out and didn't fill it in. I did the same thing the following year, but when I was 17 and the application form came through I was finally brave enough to fill it in. Even after that, when the day of the audition finally arrived I decided I didn't want to go! I was lying in bed refusing to get up, and it was my mom who basically told me I had to and made me get dressed and get out the door.

I think I was scared of being rejected, so when I kept getting through to the next stage it was just crazy. I thought they were only putting me through for a joke and that people were laughing at how bad I was.

The *X Factor* experience has been like a whirlwind, and when you're in the middle of it it's so hard to process it properly. Everything is going so fast and you're suddenly standing on red carpets and meeting famous people and singing to millions. When I look back on it now I realize how hard it was. We had very little sleep during the show and we were working nonstop, so I felt like I was having a spell in the army. You don't watch TV, you don't know what's going on in the outside world, and all that matters to you is the competition, so you can feel a bit detached from reality.

When I went into the show I had just finished my first year of sixth form, and my college told me that there was always a place for me if I wanted to go back. But as soon as I started on the show I knew that was what I wanted to do. *The X Factor* changed me so much as a person. I used to be very reserved and I found it hard to talk to people I didn't know. Even when my mom used to ask me to make a doctor's appointment for myself I hated the idea of having to speak to a stranger on the phone. Now I see fans and I'll chat away happily for ages. The show gave me a lot more confidence and taught me how to speak to people, and I'm really grateful for that.

As a band we're really close, but in some ways we're still getting to know each other a bit better every day. The first time we all properly bonded following the show was when we went to Harry's stepdad's house. But looking back, we didn't even know each other that well then. We'd been given this amazing opportunity to become a group, but the first thing that went through my mind after the excitement wore off was "how the hell are we going to organize this when we're all from different places?" Luckily Louis and Harry are a bit more organized than I am, so they came up with the plan of meeting and staying in Cheshire because it was quite easy for everyone to get to.

All the guys turned up to meet each other, and I didn't arrive until three days later because I had some family things going on at home. As soon as I got there it became evident that when you don't know people, spending three days together as they already had makes a *big* difference, so I did feel quite out of the loop and it was a bit weird at first.

Luckily a lot of the guys are really outgoing and fun, so I soon felt like a part of the group. We'd sit around a campfire singing and watch TV and eat. We were kind of getting to know each other without even realizing that we were getting to know each other.

OUR IDEA OF A
HARMONY WAS
FIVE BOYS SINGING
TOGETHER AT THE
SAME TIME

I bonded with Louis really quickly because he's like me in a lot of ways, but I also had the most arguments with him for the same reason. Harry is a cheeky chappie, so I got along well with him, but Liam was probably the person I got on best with because he's quite serious and focused. I soon realized that Niall was a bit crazy. He's so much fun and he never stops. It must be exhausting being him.

We were supposed to be rehearsing as a band during that break, but we didn't have a clue what we were doing. Most of us had been singing solo before, so this was totally different. Our idea of a harmony was five boys singing together at the same time. We were also singing things we thought were cool like Jason Derulo and Jay Sean, but they were completely wrong for us.

To be fair, we were just trying things out back then. It wasn't like we were thinking, "We're going to go and be a famous boy band" – we just wanted to try and get through Judges' Houses. We did talk a bit about staying together afterwards even if it didn't work out, but I didn't try and think too far ahead because I wanted to do everything one stage at a time. Every time we got a bit further it was another massive achievement and brought us closer together.

Judges' Houses in Marbella was probably the time when we actually felt like a group. It was the first time we auditioned as a band and sang in front of Simon, so we really pulled together.

That trip to Spain was the first time I'd been abroad, and we were in one of the nicest places ever, so I'll never forget being there. I didn't own a passport before the show. In fact, I'd never even been to London before my audition. The farthest from home I'd been was Birmingham, to go shopping, so I experienced a lot of new things very quickly.

I found Judges' Houses pretty full-on, as we did loads of filming and rehearsing, so even though we weren't supposed to go out Louis and I were a bit mischievous and snuck out a few times just to get away from things. We went to this restaurant and got some amazing pizza and sat on the beach and ate it and chatted. You could see the beach from our hotel room and it was the most incredible thing to me – I'd never seen anything like it. I just remember laughing my way through our time in Spain. It was amazing.

Getting through Judges' Houses and knowing I would be moving out of home into the contestants' house was so weird. I'd never stayed away from home for longer than a few days before. I think it was hardest on my mom because I was her only boy and she didn't want me to leave. She still cries every time I go home and then leave again. I have to say to her, "Mom, I'm not going to war, I'm just going to work."

It was hard saying goodbye to everyone and moving into this brand new house. I'd never shared a room before and all of a sudden I'm with four other guys in a tiny room with bunk beds. It soon became pretty horrible. It smelled like five teenage boys and it was so messy. I'm quite organized and I like to know where things are – that must be the womanly influence – but most of the other boys just didn't care and they'd throw things everywhere. There would be socks all over the floor, underwear hanging from light bulbs and dirty plates. It wasn't nice.

I had four bags with me and I kept them organized at all times. I had washing bags and bags for clean clothes, and they'd be at the bottom of the bed along with my shoes in a row. Louis was the worst for messiness. He'd take his clothes off to go to bed at night and just drop them on the floor. Then in the morning he'd get up, stand all over them, get new clothes out of the wardrobe and leave the other ones for days. Imagine eight weeks of that. Liam and I would clean the room sometimes, but a few days later it would be in exactly the same state again, so it was pretty pointless.

Having said that, a lot of the best memories I have from *The X Factor* were of inside the house. We used to have such a laugh playing games and eating

IT'S A BIT LIKE BEING ON THE TRUMAN SHOW SOMETIMES

together. Also, being on a red carpet for the first time was pretty cool. I wouldn't say it was one of the best memories, but it was definitely one of the weirdest. I'd never seen famous people and all the hype that goes with it. If I'd seen a famous person in the past I would never have asked for an autograph or anything, so it was strange seeing how much fuss there was around people. I guess that's why I find it so odd when people want my autograph, because I'm just me.

I'm handling being in the spotlight alright, though. I love the fans and the support we get from people, it's just strange for people to know who I am without me having to go up and introduce myself. People think they know you already because they've seen you on TV growing through the *X Factor* experience. It's a bit like being on *The Truman Show* sometimes. People think they're your friend before they know you, but people are always really nice so I'm always happy to talk.

Meeting Robbie Williams on the show was amazing. I have to admit I wasn't a massive fan before, because I wasn't into that kind of music, but I was totally converted as soon as I met him. He's got an aura about him and it's very evident when he walks into a room. He was so cool and down to earth, and while everyone else had Rihanna, Christina Aguilera and Will.i.am singing with them, Robbie stayed with us all day and got to know us. That's why you could feel the chemistry on stage.

You know when you watch a performance and you get goose pimples? Singing with Robbie was like that but magnified ten times over. I had a smile from ear to ear, and when I'm a granddad I can show my grandchildren the video and feel so proud.

One of the saddest times of the competition for me was when my granddad passed away. He was your typical happy chappie and he was constantly joking around and smiling. I have such good memories of him from when I was growing up, and I always will have.

He had been ill for a while and he'd had a few strokes, so in a way I knew it was coming. He was in a lot of pain and he was suffering, so it was probably for the best in some ways, if you can say that.

It was horrible not being at home around the time it all happened, but I was so glad that he got to see us sing "You Are So Beautiful" on the show – it was his favorite song. He said that he wanted that version played at his funeral, and it was, which was very emotional but really lovely. All of the boys came down to the funeral to support me, and it was so nice to be with them at that time. It really helped having them there.

CHRISTMAS CHEER

After the show ended, it was back to normality because we all headed home for Christmas. No one in my family treated me differently, and they're still the same even now.

It was strange for me, though, because *The X Factor* was always a Christmas thing for us. We'd watch it all the way through as a family and talk about it. I remember watching it with my mom the year Alexandra and JLS went head to head and then seeing Joe McElderry win. Now I'd actually been on it.

Thankfully nothing else had changed about Christmas. I still got up, got my presents, had dinner … just the usual. I got an iPad, which I was so chuffed with, and also shower gel and aftershave and all the usual things that teenage boys get. I was able to treat my family too because I had a bit of money. I got my sisters nice presents and I got my mom some jewelry. It was really nice to be able to do that.

Everyone in the family was incredibly supportive. Sometimes my mom or dad would talk about the show and ask what would be coming next. I know they missed me being at home because I was always such a family guy. Going out never interested me, I was happiest at home with my family, so I know it feels weird for them that I'm not around.

My friends Anthony and Danny haven't changed a bit either. They don't even think about me being in the band. They still say I can go and stay with them whenever I want to and we'll play Xbox. They don't want anything from me.

I think some of my extended family find it hard because they don't want to seem like they've changed. If they do something for me they don't want me to think they're doing it just because I'm in the band, when actually it's the same things they've always done for me. Fame can do funny things to people's minds and people sometimes overcompensate when they don't need to.

The only time I really noticed a difference over Christmas was when I took my older sister shopping for her present. She'd always wanted a pair of Uggs but we'd never been able to afford them, so we went into Leeds to look for some. I didn't realize how recognizable I had become, but literally one person clocked me and the next thing the entire shopping center came to a standstill. There was a line of people waiting to take photos of me and I was like "What the hell is going on?" My sister found it really weird as well, because I'm just her little brother! Sometimes I think it's even harder for your family to get their heads around it than it is for you.

I appreciate getting to spend time with my family so much more now, because when I do go home it's so fleeting that I make the most of every minute. That's what made Christmas so nice. We all spent as much time together as we could and we had a brilliant time.

I stayed in touch with the boys a lot over Christmas. We were like big girls, saying, "I miss you. Are you okay? What are you up to? Love you." We had spent so much time together that it felt weird to be apart. It was like being away from my family all over again in a way.

Not many fans came around over Christmas – I don't think they knew where I lived – but since then there have been quite a few things posted through the letterbox and on Valentine's Day loads of stuff got delivered. There have also been some girls shouting up at my sister's bedroom window because they thought it was mine, but I think generally my family have been able to get on with things pretty much as normal.

Interestingly, a few girls from school who were always the popular ones are now being very friendly towards me. I used to do alright with the girls anyway, but I still had to make an effort. Not any more. It does make you realize what the fame card does for you, but I'm very aware who is good for me and who isn't and I know who I can trust.

Christmas was kind of a double celebration for me and the boys because we knew we'd got a record deal, which was just incredible. Once we came off stage after finding out we came in third in *The X Factor* we were all in a bit of a state. I told myself I wasn't going to cry, but I looked over at Harry and he was with his mom crying his eyes out and that set me off. Harry and I were hugging and full-on sobbing. Someone said to us: "This isn't the end, this is just the beginning." But we had no idea what was going to happen.

I think as much as anything we were crying because the show was coming to an end. We were used to the safety and security of it and knowing what we were going to be doing each day, and all of a sudden it was over. That part of our lives was finished, even if our career wasn't.

Niall was also in tears, but Louis was trying to make us feeling better by saying we'd be okay. Liam was being level-headed about it. He's been told "no" a few times before, so he was kind of used to it, but we were all gutted.

We got called up to Simon's dressing room and then came a classic Simon moment. We all sat there and he was looking at us and it felt like we were back at Judges' Houses again. Then all of a sudden he said: "You were great on the show. Sony are going to sign you up in the morning." Harry started crying again and we sat there in absolute shock. Simon hugged us all and said: "You're going to be alright, don't worry about coming third." Then we all went back downstairs to the bar. We were allowed to tell our families but no one else, and we were on such a high.

We played a lot of gigs once the series finished and it was all new for me. I'd never even been to a nightclub before, although my friends used to go, so it was yet another new experience for me.

In all fairness I lived a very quiet, boring and sheltered life before the band. I enjoyed the simple things, like being at home in my room playing computer games, so absolutely everything that happened was a learning curve.

I loved doing gigs right from the start. I loved the buzz of being on stage and seeing the fans. The reaction we got was unbelievable. The under 18s nights were mad, but after the first few times we knew what to expect.

PLANS AND PLAY

I knew that by the time New Year's Eve rolled around I'd be wanting to celebrate everything that had happened. I planned on staying in with my friends and

having a few drinks and a quiet night, but it didn't quite work out like that. As I've said before I've never been one for going out a lot, but if there was ever a time to go out and have fun, this was it. Funnily enough I got invited to a lot of parties by people – some I didn't even know that well.

My friends were up for going out and in the end we had a bit of a crazy night and I woke up on someone's bathroom floor. I got up and walked home and it was the first time I'd felt normal for ages. After getting so used to being in cars all of the time it was nice to be out in the fresh air, just wandering along on my own.

After New Year's I headed back down to London. Once again it was hard saying goodbye to everyone, but I was excited about what 2011 would bring. We had a meeting to discuss our schedule for the year, which looked amazingly busy. It was difficult to get our heads around how much we had going on.

We all moved into a hotel, and we've basically moved around different hotels ever since. We're all planning to get our own places but there just hasn't been time yet. We did talk about all living together, but as we spend every minute together anyway we decided it might not be the best idea. Liam wants to move in with his friend, and Harry's moving in with Louis. But Niall's full-on and I'm quiet so we agreed we were better not moving in together. There was no drama; we were just totally honest about it. So we're both looking for our own places now.

It's going to be a big thing for me moving into a new place in a new area on my own. Up till now I've never lived in London, I've never lived on my own and I've obviously never been famous, so I'm kind of doing everything at once. But it will be nice to live out of a wardrobe again instead of a suitcase. I have gotten very good at packing, but it's much more comforting when you knew where everything is and you've got a base, so having a place will make a big difference.

I THINK AS MUCH AS ANYTHING WE WERE CRYING BECAUSE THE SHOW WAS COMING TO AN END

We spent most of January either doing gigs or starting work on the album in various recording studios. For me, the best part of being in the band is the time we spend in the studio. I love the whole lifestyle of us all hanging out together and ordering in pizza! The studio is much more fun when you're in a band because you've always got someone to mess around, play games and do some writing with. We're co-writing a lot of the album, which I love because I've always been into writing poetry. To me writing a song is the same as writing poetry, with a melody in the background. Studio life for me is perfect.

In February we headed to LA to do some work on the album, which was absolutely crazy. It's a different world out there, though at one point I was worried I wasn't even going to get into the country. All the other guys went through passport control fine, then a woman stopped me, called over our tour manager Paul and said: "There's a problem with him. He needs to go in the back." They took me into a room and I thought they were going to keep me there for hours, but thankfully the women who came to talk to me knew who Simon Cowell was and knew I was in a band. In the end I was interviewed for an hour about what I was doing there and why I was visiting America. It turned out that my name was flagged up as similar to that of someone they were looking for, so they were just being cautious. I got stopped at customs as well, but again I got through okay as the guy there was really nice. It was then that LA really began for me.

Everything in LA is so much bigger than in the UK. The roads are about five times the size, and even a regular takeout is like a large over here. A large is like a bucket. When we arrived at the hotel this man greeted us at the door saying: "Oh my god, the boys are here. Whaddup? Come inside." People were walking along the street giving out water and telling you to have a nice day. Can you imagine anyone doing that in the UK? Everything seems sugar coated over there.

Being in the studio there and recording with the RedOne team was brilliant because they're so famous and have worked with so many massive artists. But they were just nice, normal guys. The weather was warm and sunny, so we were in t-shirts and shorts and loving every minute of it. We went out to eat quite a lot.

We also did a lot of shopping over there. I love high-top sneakers and I bought loads of pairs because they're so much cheaper there. They even cover sneakers in cling film so you can't damage them when you pick them up, and I love the fact they have so much respect for their sneakers. I've always treated my sneakers well. I used to keep all of mine in boxes to keep them looking nice.

I bought a pair of limited edition, black Nike high tops that cost me around $300. I know it's a lot but they're amazing. They've sat at home in my wardrobe because I'm too scared to wear them.

I'm getting more used to traveling now. I hated flying the first time when we went to Spain, but now I don't mind it at all. I did miss England a bit, though. I had a brilliant time and I'm looking forward to going away again, but I did feel happy when we landed back in the UK. But then we had the craziest experience when we got back to Heathrow. We were told that there were about 200 people waiting for us, so we were ready to sign autographs and things. But when we walked out this whole swarm of people came towards us, so we had to run back inside the airport. There was no plan, so we just held on to each other and ran. We only had Paul, our tour manager with us, as well as some of the airport security, so we just had to go for it. There must have been about 600 to 700 girls and my t-shirt and hair were pulled, and Louis had half of his hoodie ripped off. We ran into a car parking booth and locked the door and all these girls were outside the glass, looking in at us. It was a bit like a zombie film. In the end Paul had to call a police riot van and get us out. It was the most hectic thing I've ever been through in my life.

THIS IS IT!

The tour rehearsals for the *X Factor* tour went surprisingly well for me – even the dancing. My confidence has improved so much since Bootcamp and I can have much more of a laugh with the boys about it all. I ended up really enjoying it and we learned so much. We were really excited when we heard we were going on the tour, and it was as great as we hoped. It was like being on the show, but not as crazy. We got time off to shop, we got a chance to have a lie-in, and we got to hang out together and eat nice food. Then every night we got to go on stage and be pop stars. I honestly can't think of anything better than that.

The reaction we got was unbelievable, and people of all ages were screaming at us all and having the best time. A year ago the thought of being on stage in front of that many people would have been enough to make me physically sick, but now I go out and walk around the stage and I feel so much more confident. It's absolutely the best feeling.

We weren't very demanding on the tour at all. In the dressing room shared by all the male performers we had a little basket which was filled with sweets, drinks, chips and fruit, but that was it. It was great sharing a room with the other guys from the show and getting to hang out with people like Aiden and Matt, because I love those guys. Aiden is a lot like me. He's quite laid-back and reserved and we get on really well. I got on well with Wagner too. He's very funny and has so many stories to tell. He kept everyone entertained and I used to make time just to hear his stories. In my eyes he's a living legend.

We had quite a few hotel parties on tour. There was always a private bar where we could chill out and chat after shows, so that was a good time to catch up with people. It was nice doing things like that, and also just being myself and playing games. We all got our own rooms, so if we wanted to have time to ourselves, we could. So sometimes after shows I'd head to my room and chill out. I need that. Having time alone is how I keep myself sane.

PRESS ATTENTION SCARES ME A BIT AS WELL. I WORRY ABOUT BEING SEEN AS A BAD PERSON

Ireland was one of my favorite places to visit on the tour. They absolutely love *The X Factor* over there. Getting to play Wembley was wicked as well. I'd happily go on tour again tomorrow.

To me the most surprising thing about fame so far is that you don't realize how recognizable you are. Louis and I wanted to go out the other night, but there was just no way as there were loads of people around, and if there's more than one of you it's much more likely you'll get spotted. I went to the supermarket with my mom recently and because I wore a hat and glasses I didn't get recognized until after I'd left. So there are ways around it if you're on your own and you do want a quiet time.

It's so weird because I'll forget about everything and then someone will be like "It's you." And I'm thinking, "I'm just Zayn Malik, that kid from Bradford who used to stay in his room and play on the computer all the time."

Press attention scares me a little bit as well. I worry about being seen as a bad person. Everyone makes mistakes, but when you're famous it's plastered everywhere. I don't quite know how to deal with everything yet. I want to be open, but I'm still learning about how open I can be and who I can trust totally.

The maddest things have happened to us since the band kicked off. Rio Ferdinand's invited us to his restaurant, we've got our own merchandise coming out, and we also filmed a Nintendo ad. We filmed it in a lovely hotel in London and it wasn't at all forced, it was just us lot messing around and playing on DS and having a laugh. We had so many things happening, before we had even released our album, which was mad. We could not be more excited about making music and having it out there.

We had been looking forward to getting a book released, and when so many people went out and bought the first one and came along to book signings it made us realize how many fans we had. There wasn't a dull moment during the

signings and we got masses of presents. We got chocolates and roses, and Liam even got some Play-Doh!

The book signings were some of the earliest promotional things we did, and we also did some photo shoots for various things, which I don't mind at all because I'm a bit of a poser. We also went on the Alan Titchmarsh show, and that was even weirder for me than being on *The X Factor*. That whole experience had been such a blur, but this felt much more real and it really hit home that we were known and kind of famous.

The weirdest thing was when the Nintendo ad came on. I was at my friends' house and seeing us on TV was crazy. I've only really got two close friends, Danny and Anthony; they love the fact that I'm famous and we stay in touch all the time.

We started working on the documentary earlier in the year. We didn't find it nearly as strange as we thought we would, probably because we'd had cameras following us around all of the time on *The X Factor* and we'd been thrown in at the deep end back then. We'd had a lot of experience, so we didn't freeze in front of the cameras, we were just ourselves. When you're used to it you soon forget that the cameras are there. We just got on with it really, so what people see is what really happened.

The wrap party for the tour was an interesting one. Quite a few people were boogying and getting down, but I had a flight to Spain early the next day so I left by midnight and went to bed. My experience of the wrap party was tame compared to some of the other guys. I was sad to see the tour end, but going on holiday was wicked.

Recording the album was fantastic for me because I love anything to do with song lyrics and recording. I'd never been to Sweden before, so going there was a totally new experience, and it was such an amazing place. We also loved getting to go back to LA, because the first time around we only got to spend five days there and we didn't see a lot. This time we were there for three weeks, so we got to go out and see more places.

It feels so strange when I look back to before *The X Factor*, when I didn't even have a passport and hadn't been outside the UK. Now all of a sudden I've been to all of these amazing places. It's weird but it's wicked as well. I enjoy flying – it's very cool.

As soon as we started recording music we were aware that people would be surprised by it, because it's not typical boy band music. There's nothing else out there like our sound at the moment. It's completely new. It's One Direction's sound and we love it.

When we found out we were going to be doing our own tour we were so happy. For the first time it's not just about *The X Factor*, it's about One Direction. We've been given the chance to shine, and really show people how much we've improved and progressed since the show.

This whole year has been really interesting and a lot of fun, and I'm excited about everything that's coming up, because there are going to be a few surprises here and there.

QUICKFIRE

DOB: 1/12/1993
STAR SIGN: Capricorn

favorite ...
BOOK: *Harry Potter*

FILM: *Freedom Writers*

BODY PART: My jaw line

FOOD: Chicken

ALBUM: Donell Jones

FRIEND: Liam Payne

CELEBRITY LADY: Megan Fox

SHOP: Topman

DRINK: Red Bull

COLOR: Red

TV SHOW: *Family Guy*

AFTERSHAVE: Unforgivable by Sean John

PERFUME: I don't know names but I like sweet ones.

COMPUTER GAME: Halo

IPHONE APP: Fat Face

WAY TO SPEND A SUNDAY: In bed

DATE VENUE: Restaurant

COUNTRY: England

RESTAURANT: Nandos

WAY TO RELAX: Chilling out in bed

MODE OF TRANSPORT: Car

NIGHT OUT: Cinema

BAND: *NSYNC

WHAT COLOR IS YOUR DUVET COVER? Black

WHAT KIND OF UNDERWEAR DO YOU WEAR? Jersey boxers

FIRST PET: A staffie dog called Tyson

DO YOU LIKE YOUR OWN COMPANY OR OTHER PEOPLE'S? I like my own company. I do like people, but I like being alone too

LAST BOOK YOU READ: *A Child Called It*

LAST FIVE THINGS YOU BOUGHT: Clothes, clothes, clothes, clothes and clothes

WHAT TYPE OF GIRLS DO YOU LIKE? Someone I can get on with. I don't have a specific type looks-wise. I want someone who I feel comfortable around and I can spoil a bit

THANKS

ONE DIRECTION: We would like to thank everyone who has helped us to reach this amazing milestone – our second book! We're extremely proud. To everyone who has supported us before we were One Direction, especially to our families and our friends – thank you.

To everyone that we have worked with in the last year, we are so incredibly grateful for your guidance, diligence, encouragement and belief. We're going to do our damnedest to make you proud!

Finally, to our fans. It's hard to avoid a cliché here, but we really wouldn't be here without you! Your generosity and love constantly surprise us. THANK YOU! X

HARRY: This year has been incredible through the *X Factor* tour and making the album, and there are some people I have to thank.

I want to thank Simon Cowell, Sonny Takhtar, Tyler Brown, Mark Hardy, Kim 'Jimmy' Davidson, Reema Chuhan, Russel Eslamafir, Simon Jones and everyone at SYCO and Sony.

A huge thank you goes to Richard Griffiths, Harry Magee, Will Bloomfield, Marco Gastel, Katie Ray, Annecka Griffiths, Emily Montgomery and everyone at Modest Management.

And thanks to Nicola Carson and Innis Ferguson for looking after us in America, and for showing us how to drink mud.

I want to thank my family for supporting me the whole time through this experience so far – my mom, dad, sister, Robin, Mike, Amy, Noel and Archie. I want to thank my cousins Matthew, Ben and Ella. And I'd like to thank my auntie and uncle, Mike and Dee. I want to thank my granddad Brian for being the coolest guy ever. And I'd like to thank and congratulate my grandma Beryl for getting to the phone in time when I call her. Thanks too to my grandparents Mary and Keith for watching over me.

I want to thank my friends for always being there for me – John, Ben, Nick, Naomi, Emilie, Ashley, Sophie, Ellis, Lydia and Will. Love seeing you guys even though it doesn't happen that much... miss you guys.

I want to thank my sister again for always understanding me being busy, but always being there to talk when I am free. I love you.

I want to say a huge thank you to our tour manager Paul Higgins – you help us with so many things and we couldn't ask for a better guy to have with us... and congratulations on your recent wedding... your wife is hot.

A big thanks to our security team, who do an incredible job at keeping us in check.

Thanks to Ali Barker and Savan for overseeing and helping us through all new things we encountered while we were making the album.

A massive thank you goes out to all the fans, whose support has been incredible... you guys are unbelievable and we wouldn't be where we are without you, so thank you so much.

I'd like to thank Alex Kadis for being the smartest person ever and being so easy to talk to... and helping me see things in different ways... she's the best "teacher."

A massive thank you to Dennis for your many words and just for being you... I'm still mulling over your words of wisdom!!

Thank you to Louis, Liam, Zayn and Niall for being so hard working and just great people... it's incredible that we choose to spend extra time with each other after the all-day sessions, haha!

I'm extremely sorry if I've missed anyone... I love you all.

LIAM: Thanks to my mom and dad for their support. Wherever I end up in the world they're always on the other end of a phone when I need them. Thanks too to my sisters Nicola and Ruth for taking me out and about when I'm bored at home and putting up with me being immature :) I'd like to re-thank all of the *X Factor* production and crew team for helping us through the whole *X Factor* experience.

I'd also like to thank a few people who helped me before all of this – Jamie from the Great Western Pub for giving me the opportunity to sing in public and have a great time doing so; Graham Lauren for many vocal lessons; Roysten, Nick and Ashley and all of their team for cutting my hair :)

To Ronnie, Paul and Hannah and their families for all their hard work and help before all this, making things fun and exciting even if I was only singing to three people in a field, haha. I'd like to thank the team that we have around us 24/7 for putting up with our madness; Preston and Ian from the security team for having a laugh with us and keeping us all smiley; and Paul for being a fantastic tour manager and for being like a big brother (didn't want to call you dad) and always being there for us to talk to if there is a problem.

Lou from hair and makeup, Caroline and Lydia from styling for making sure we look our best.

Thank you also to Vicky and the wonderful team at HarperCollins for turning our thoughts into words and for all your hard work.

All of the people who are writing songs for us – you're doing a fantastic job, I love almost everything I hear. Special thanks to Rami for writing the first single.

I'd like to thank all of our team at SYCO – Kim and Mark from marketing for coming up with all their great ideas, Sonny and Tyler from A&R for finding the best songs for us, and lastly Simon for being a great boss.

I'd like to thank Richard, Harry and Will, and Marco and Emily from management for putting us in the best position possible for the times ahead, and for putting up with our madness.

I'd like to give a big huge thank you to all of my boys for becoming the best four friends/brothers I have. You've all made this the most amazing and exciting time ever, and it would be pointless without you.

I'd lastly like to make the hugest and biggest and super-huge thank you to all our fans. No matter where we are in the world you never stop coming to show your support and we love you for it, thank you so much.

Sorry for anyone I have missed but I appreciate everything you ever did for me so don't be mad at me for missing you out!!

LOUIS: What an incredible year I've had, and I'd like to take a moment to thank every person who has made this year so special to me.

I would like to start off by saying a massive thanks to Simon, Sonny and everyone at SYCO who was involved with offering us a record contract. Ali Barker, thank you for helping us in the early stages of making the record. And of course Tyler Brown – fair play for putting up with our constant abuse and banter.

Massive thanks to the pregnant idiot that is Lou Teasdale. You're an absolute babe and have done a great job of what was a very embarrassing bowl-shaped haircut.

Modest Management have all been fantastic – special thanks to Richard and Harry and for some funny memories, one of which was dressing up in Richard's coat and massively trendy Manchester United cap. Annecka and Will were great friends during the tour but also a great laugh. Big thanks to our current manager Will Bloomfield, who get's involved with the banter. However he needs to give me a heads up when he's going to wear stripes, as it's a bit embarrassing when me and my manager have matching t-shirts. Marco, keep up the hard work and the Milan vibes.

A very special thanks to Paul Higgins, who has been a great leader, but also a great friend to all of us. And of course to Preston – thank you for letting us put our heads out of the sun-roof and drink on the job (that's obviously a joke!).

Mom, you have been my best, best friend throughout this experience, I can't thank you enough for all your help. Thank you for being so selfless and generous. I love you.

Thank you to the rest of my family and friends, especially my dad, my four lovely sisters, who are growing up so fast, both sets of my grandparents, my great nan Olive, my aunty Rach, and Stan and Hannah. Again, I would also like to thank Edna and Leonard, who were my great grandparents who I miss dearly. I know my nan would be telling everyone at line-dancing about everything, and the same for my granddad at the pub while playing dominoes. I love you all dearly.

Of course a special thanks to the KFC Colonel for giving me the opportunity to embrace the "Krushems" experience, something that will stay with me for the rest of my life. Thank you Colonel – I'm truly grateful. Also, of course, a thank you to Mecca Bingo – without such a fantastic game my life wouldn't be complete.

Massive thanks to all the fans for their continued support throughout *The X Factor*, during the tour and right through to buying our first single. We would be nothing without you, thank you so much for everything. We love you!

Finally, of course, thank you to the four boys that have kept up the laughs and jokes through this amazing experience: Harry, Liam, Zayn and Niall. I'm so lucky to have met you all.

Going through all these thank yous has made me truly grateful for everything that everyone does for me. I am incredibly lucky to have you all.

Thank you so much, guys.

NIALL: I would like to start off by saying that this has been the most amazing year of my life so far. We have been on the *X Factor* arena tour – what an amazing experience. We have been recording our first album, and during that process we have been able to travel so much; we have been to Sweden and LA, and got to work with some of the best producers in the world.

While we've been doing this, we have had help and guidance from some amazing people. I would now like to thank some of these people!

Thanks to our amazing tour manager, the one and only Paul Higgins, who comes everywhere with us and is with us 24/7. Without you we would be goosed, you are a top guy (obviously being Irish plays a big part in that...). Big thanks also to all our other security lads.

I would also like to thank our general manager Will Bloomfield and his assistant Marco Gastel, who have been amazing with us. Will's knowledge of the industry is endless and he is always there if we need a helping hand! Thanks also to everyone at Modest Management, the backbone behind this whole process: Richard and Harry, Katie Day, Ben Evans, and Nicola Carson – our manager in the US. Thanks for being there for us and helping us out. Can't thank you guys enough.

Thanks to everyone at SYCO music, especially our A&R consultants and marketing managers.

Thanks to all the people who have taken in this year with us. It's been wild and we are so grateful for everything that has happened to us and the people we have met.

I'd also like to say thank you to the amazing producers and songwriters we have worked with: the one and only Savan Kotecha, who has stuck with us since the show and wrote some of our tracks with us, Steve Robson, Wayne Hector, Steve Mac, Jamie Scott, all the guys at Metrophonic, Rami Yacoub, RedOne and all the guys, Andrew Frampton, Kojak ("Everyday I'm Stackin' It, Stack It Real Hard"), Claude Kelly, Andreas and Josef at Quiz Larossi, Matt Squire and Toby Gad. It was an amazing experience working with all these guys.

Major, major thank you to our incredible fans worldwide. We would literally be nothing without you and we appreciate every single one of you guys, you have been amazing everywhere we go, on tour, on the street, at our book signings, and of course on Twitter and Facebook, where we try our best to keep you connected with our day-to-day lives. We promise to keep you up to date on what we know, we love you so much and we hope you stick with us!

A massive thank you to the lads – Harry, Zayn, Liam and Louis – for making this year the best year of my life, all the laughs and banter and messing about... and then the general friendship we have together... literally my four best friends... love you loads, lads...

Thank you so much to everyone again! It's been great working alongside you to make us what we are today: One Direction.

lots of love

Nialler

ZAYN: This year has been a memorable one and I would like to thank all the people that helped to make it that way.

I also want to say I've had a lot of fun with the four other boys this year and hopefully there are many more years to come :)

I would like to thank my family and friends, who have supported me and always had faith in me. I would also like to thank Modest Management for helping me with this amazing opportunity I've been given, and Simon and his record label SYCO for giving me the opportunity :)